Perspectives for Architecture

Georg Schaarwächter

Perspectives for Architecture

Frederick A. Praeger, Publishers, New York · Washington

BOOKS THAT MATTER

Published in the United States of America in 1967
by Frederick A. Praeger, Inc., Publishers
111 Fourth Avenue, New York, N. Y. 10003
Copyright 1964 by Verlag Gerd Hatje, Stuttgart
Library of Congress Catalog Card Number: 67-20404
Printed in Germany

Translated into English by E. R. Dawson

Contents

The formation and meaning of the abbreviations used

Capital letters generally denote points, small letters straight lines or intervals. Two capital letters side by side, joined by a dash, also denote an interval. Greek letters (α, β, etc.) denote angles.
Literal subscripts or primes are used to give a more precise significance to other letters.

Examples

1. Subscripts
h_a	Height above the horizon
h_b	Height below the horizon
V_r	Vanishing point right
V_l	Vanishing point left
M_r	Measuring point for vanishing point right
M_l	Measuring point for vanishing point left
V_v	Vertical vanishing point
M_v	Measuring point for verticals

2. Primes
P	Point
P′	Foot of perpendicular
P″	Shadow point
h	horizon
h′, h″	vanishing traces

The most important abbreviations
SP	Station point
S	Standpoint
h_e	Height of eye = the interval S to SP
PP	Picture plane
h	Horizon
CV	Centre of vision
D	Diagonal point or distance point
d	Distance = interval SP to CV
	= interval CV to D
V	Vanishing point
g	Ground line or floor trace, at a distance h_e below h
d l	depth line
h_r	room height, roof height
M	Measuring point
L, S_o	Light point, sun point

The type of perspective used by architects is linear perspective. This theory of representation develops into a number of equivalent processes which enable what has been planned but not yet built to be depicted as it will appear at some future time. How to draw the picture most accurately and quickly depends on the particular thing to be represented. This book provides examples of all the usual methods.

Perspective drawing is easy. It is based on a few constantly recurring considerations and consists in using certain auxiliary lines, almost always straight. But, of course, if something complicated has to be accurately represented, the work must be done carefully and patiently.

To explain them to the reader as clearly as possible, all the important processes are shown in detail in all their stages. In each case, what is new strikes the eye; even if the student is working without a teacher, he will easily assimilate the material. The text and diagrams are complementary; references to previous explanations are minimized for the reader's convenience, even though this leads to a certain amount of repetition. A more abstract treatment would have been possible and would have reduced the size of the book, but would have made more demands on the reader, particularly to combine the various constructions. The examples simplify the presentation.

The brief preliminary notes on simple constructions with ruler and compasses should serve as a supplement and a suitable introduction to the theory of perspective. The book deals solely with the representation of rectilinear outlines. It does not deal with the drawing of people, animals, or plants, nor with free-hand drawing, charcoal drawing, pen or brush work, the use of foils, colours, stencils, or spray-painting techniques. Much as all these can heighten effects, it would be only diversionary to discuss them here.

Perspective drawing is only an ancillary tool for the architect. But perspective insight, the ability to 'see every aspect' of a design, to grasp the definitive and the subordinate viewpoints—precise vision, in fact—this is part and parcel of the art of building, to which perhaps this book too may make its contribution.

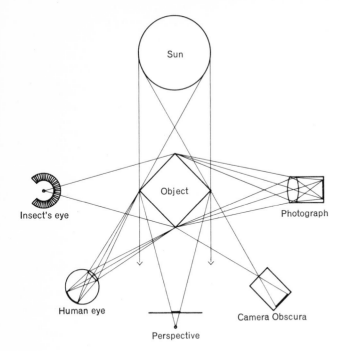

Sun

Insect's eye

Object

Photograph

Human eye

Perspective

Camera Obscura

Our word 'perspective' is derived, via the Italian, from the late Latin *perspectivus*, from *perspicere*, to look through, to view. The use of certain perspective instruments may have led to the idea of looking *through* instead of looking *at*, of looking *into* a picture instead of looking *at* a picture. Probably it was the Renaissance conviction that a perspective is not simply a view but the only correct and proper one, the most soundly based and the closest to reality, the 'best of all possible representations of the world'.

Since that age this conviction has been profoundly shaken. The routine labour of a draughtsman in drawing a perspective according to prescribed rules has been reduced by the automatic, physico-chemical processes of the photographer, just as the routine labour of a human computer has been reduced by automatic processes in electronic brains. The architect recalls his knowledge of perspective acquired in the schools only if his client fails to comprehend all the plans proposed and if it would be too expensive to make models and photograph them. Nor do artists seem to want to know about perspective any more. They consider it useless and superfluous in its simplest form, justifying their attitude by the fact that, until the Renaissance, no artist in the world had ever used perspective.

To say that they did not use it because they had not got it to use would be too facile an answer: for there are some tasks and purposes, some modes of representation, which do not admit the use of perspective.

Vision and Perception

The world casts its reflection at us; our eyes form an image of it, making an ordered selection. We have only a general awareness of the greatest part of our field of vision. Only the point at which we are momentarily looking—an area about the size of a thumbnail held at arm's length—appears clearly. For everything else, even in the same line of vision, the lens of the eye has to change shape and the axis of the eye has to be properly adjusted; that is why we can so easily overlook animals in the open air against the background. Many people have defective vision, either inborn or arising from overstrain, illness, or old age; some are colour-blind, short-sighted, or long-sighted. Even healthy eyes prove slow and unreliable in changes between light and dark. Strong images persist on the retina when brightness and colours change; the illusion of 'flying saucers' may, for instance, have been produced in this way.

Just as in all the various projections—in plan, elevation, or in axonometric or perspective drawing—quite different objects may have the same representation, so quite different objects, real or imaginary, living or dead, solid or flat, may seem exactly the same to our eyes. It is difficult to estimate how often our understanding, which alone provides the insight in addition to mere 'seeing', is deceived by such similarities. In the case of pictures it is usually immediately clear that they only represent and hint at reality. But the hints suffice to fire our imagination.

Historical

When the Vizier Imhotep in about 2800 BC planned and executed buildings on a grand scale for the Pharaoh Zoser, he may in fact have conceived the 'step pyramid' of Sakkara as a representation of the hierarchy of the land. And at a later date King Cheops portrayed by his pyramid the 'great unity' of his people. Perspective was unthinkable there. A pyramid was a vast symbol to all; a perspective applies to precisely one single person, to the optimally placed observer. To him everything appears according to the principle 'foreground large, background small'. At court, on the other hand, size depends on office and dignity, on the amount of respect or dread inspired. Sizes in Egyptian wall reliefs vary consistently with the grade of authority portrayed. There could be no question of perspective.

The first great Greek painter whose name has come down to us, Polygnotus of Thasos, drew gods and heroes in elevation, so to speak; the figures were detached and seldom overlapping, ranged in two or three rows one above the other, and the farther were not smaller nor dimmer than the nearer. His style must have been similar to that of the vase paintings which have come down to us. But not long afterwards, at the time of Pericles, the artists Agatharchos and Apollodoros painted deceptively naturally, which means that they must have known at least the simple rules of perspective. At first derided, they later gained remarkable renown. The really extraordinary naturalness of their paintings was not, of course, to everyone's liking. Aristotle saw in it a decline from idealism, a renunciation of the grand style, of stability and the deeper underlying significance, a turning towards the superficialities of representational art. As if to prove him right, all that has survived of this whole period of Grecian painting is its fame and a later resplendence in the ruins of Pompeii.

The wall paintings in Pompeii mark a peak of culture and   8 civilization, of grace and genius; and a surprisingly skilful use of perspective is revealed in their workmanship. Admittedly, the perspectives are not quite right; it is said that the mathematical principles were unknown. This is a bit unfair, since, strictly speaking, it is quite impossible to cover walls like those in Pompeii completely with perspectives. But the difficulties seemed to be insoluble even in smaller pictures. So they contented themselves with what was almost right or they turned to something different, to the stylized décor which was more splendid and easier to carve or produce in mosaic.

Christianity itself brought no change. There was no need for the systematic use of perspective in the presentation of the Church's requirements. It developed only at the end of the Middle Ages when artists in Flanders, Burgundy, and Italy wanted to paint rooms and buildings. The van Eyck brothers, Filippo Brunelleschi (the architect of the cupola of the cathedral of Santa Maria del Fiore in Florence), the all-round genius Leone Battista Alberti (1404–1472), all assisted its progress, and Piero della Francesca (1420–1472) wrote the first textbook on it. Central perspective with all its possibilities had already been tried out before 1500.

Perspective building, perspective painting, even the textbooks on perspective flourished in the Baroque age. It was in the Baroque era too that Europe for the first time became closely acquainted with the art of China. This style of painting, despite its great naturalness, lacks proper perspective. This is an inevitable result of Chinese custom. In China, pictures are kept rolled up and are unrolled only when they are to be looked at. Roll pictures can best be handled when they are rolled as long strips round short rods. There are cross-rolls to be rolled from one hand to the other, and also hanging rolls. When we look at horizontal rolls, our station point moves across. Thus the hypothesis on which a perspective drawing is based fails completely. If a tall, narrow, hanging picture were drawn perspectively, there would be an intolerable amount of distortion at the top and bottom, unless the standpoint had been chosen to be so far removed that the picture approximated to a parallel projection (vertical axonometry). This fact conditions the mode of representation in detail in almost all Chinese pictures. The picture is loosely made up of separate motifs, each of its own size and with its own direction of projection. Remotely similar to these pictures are some of our rococo ceiling paintings, composed of several parts, each a perspective with its own centre of vision. To people of the nineteenth century such systems appeared too artificial, too intricate, and yet at the same time insufficiently accurate. They developed photography.

Is perspective now superfluous?

Nowadays almost everyone who has anything to do with perspectives has already taken a photograph. Photographic apparatus has evolved from the so-called *camera obscura*, which was described by Della Porta in 1558, though its principle may already have been used in the time of Belshazzar in Babylon. A hole in the front face of an otherwise closed box allows a cone of daylight to enter and to form on the back flat surface of the box a weak, inverted and reversed image of objects situated outside the box opposite the hole. If we think of the direction of the rays of light before they enter the hole, we can speak of a double cone of rays. In photographic apparatus the hole of the camera obscura has been replaced by bigger and bigger lens systems which intensify the image without altering it, but which unfortunately form a really clear-cut image of a smaller and smaller space. In a perspective the path of the rays is different; they form a single cone which is, however, cut off by the picture plane before the rays reach their vertex. Nevertheless it can be demonstrated that photographs, camera obscura images, and perspective drawings are produced according to the same laws and can be seen together, so that we can without difficulty draw perspectives on to photographs or stick corresponding photographs, except 'fish-eye' views, into a perspective drawing.

Photography, the daughter of perspective and the Proteus of technology, has with its ever brighter and more colourful development entirely thrust its mother back into the restricted domain of portraying future or Utopian architecture.

So we should recall the real power of perspective.

Correct vanishing points are good; correct standpoints are better.

Brilliant artist's impressions may be beautiful, but proper perspectives drawn in advance are more reliable. Perspective provides—at the right time—the opportunity for critical examination of one's designs.

Recommendations regarding Materials

Drawing–Board
To be of knot-free poplar, suitable for standard size (A 2) paper, but if possible larger, e.g. 1.00 m. × 1.50 m. (3 ft. 6 in. × 5 ft.); must be plane, smooth, clean, and have straight edges.

Cardboard Cover
Serves to rest on while drawing and to protect the board. A large sheet of cardboard is placed on the drawing-board so as to leave its shorter side free for the use of the T-square; the cardboard is moistened uniformly in the evening, is bent round the long edges of the drawing-board, and its two ends are fastened or glued together. Next morning this cardboard sheath will be ready for use.

Paper
Transparent paper, weight 34–38 lb. per double-crown ream (so that it will not easily tear under the eraser), in rolls or sheets; should be carefully protected from damp. White cartridge paper; should be free from wood, otherwise it fades; Indian ink should not spread out on it. Waste paper and thin transparent paper for rough sketches and for covering completed parts of a drawing.

Fastenings
Adhesive strips in film or crêpe form, possibly in tear-off containers, usable up to three times.
Proper drawing-board pins, with wedge-shaped, smooth pins without rough edges, gently arched heads, which when pressed fully home will hold the paper round their rims. The corners of the drawing paper should be secured diagonally, not going round the corners in turn. Cheap drawing-pins ruin one's fingernails and the drawing-board.

T-squares
At least 70 cm. (27 in.) long. Beechwood T-squares tend to become rough; transparent plastic ones are usually too flexible.

Set-squares
Of 30° and 45° angle, the shorter side about 20 cm. (8 in.) long, made of transparent plastic, without gradations (they shrink), preferably with both sides bevelled (for use with Indian ink). Care must be taken when drawing that the set-square does not slide under the edge of the T-square or of another set-square.

French Curves
Of transparent plastic, rigid, with bevelled edges for use with ink.

Rulers
Of white plastic, 30 cm. (12 in.) long (not longer) with millimetre subdivisions (half-millimetre gradations are hard to read), with a ridge for holding it firm; gradations on both sides.

Laths
Not more than 3 mm. ($^1/_8$ in.) thick, of straight, waxed, first-class pinewood, for vanishing lines and large circles.

Drawing stylus
Lead holder of solid sheet metal, able to hold all kinds of leads, with leads of hardness 2H or 4H.

Leads

For rough sketches: quite soft, say 6B.
For technical sketches: soft, B.
For drawings; hard, 4H.
For 'blue-print' drawings; medium, H.
A good point is 1–1.5 cm ($^1/_3$–$^2/_3$ in.) long and needle sharp.

Abrasive strips for pointing leads
Rotate the lead when sharpening it; use coarse, fine, and polishing abrasive strips. It is best to sharpen the lead into a tin, and also to keep the abrasive strips in a tin. There is now available a very convenient lead pointing device using interchangeable rotary cutters.

Drawing Instruments
Compasses, with extension pieces for large circles, with insertions for divider points, lead, or ink drawings.
Spring bow-compasses or adjustable compasses for very small circles or for drawing several circles all of the same size.
Drawing pen with fixed holder.
High-quality instruments are essential. The compasses should draw a sharp circle without waviness or 'chatter' even under pressure; the holding clamps should be adjustable. The blades of the nibs must always be the same length, rounded off, knife sharp, and be kept clean from 'whiskers' or ink deposits. Sharpen them on a fine instrument hone or if necessary on a fine emery abrasive strip. Slack screws should be tightened; eraser dust should be kept out of the drawing-instrument box.

Drawing Pen ('Graphos')
For use with Indian ink; should be openable for cleaning and filling; large selection of nibs—here A 0.1, A 0.2, A 0.4 will suffice for drawings, and O 0.2 for small lettering. Indian ink dries very quickly. Instruments should be cleaned with rag when the work is finished or during any pause. The nibs must have the Indian ink only on the inside, and so they cannot be dipped in. Hold the pen slightly inclined against the edge of a set-square or T-square to prevent blots forming on the underside when drawing. If the ink stops running, touch the nib gently against a damp sponge.

Pins
These are used to fix the vanishing points, points of rotation, or foci. To avoid damage to the drawing-board, however, it is better to use instead of these small flat bits of metal with a sharp vertical edge to act as the vanishing point pivot.

Rings of elastic thread
The need for continual care to see that the drawing edge is in contact with the pin marking a vanishing point can be avoided by using an elastic thread or gummed paper strip to keep the lath in contact with the pin.

Razor blades
For erasing Indian ink; complete the erasure with a typewriter eraser, and to prevent spreading at the erased point rub with the fingernail or a lead pencil.

Erasers
For hard lines use a typewriter eraser, for soft lines use a soapy rubber, and for dust use a draughtsman's crumbly eraser. For small erasures an erasing mask may be used; erasure dust should be swept off with a handbrush into a waste-paper basket.

Matchstick
Usually drawing paper is cut off using a guillotine or a large pair of paper shears. The T-square edge should never be used as a guide for cutting paper; nor the drawing-board as the platform. Use instead a steel edge with a sheet of glass below the paper. But if need be, it is possible to stick the corner of a razor blade through a matchstick and then a T-square can be used since its edge will be protected by the matchstick.

Lighting
Should be from the left or from in front; a north aspect is best, since sunshine easily dazzles. Lamps should be clampable and adjustable with powerful bulbs. When fluorescent lighting is used, attention should be paid to its colour and there should be no hum.

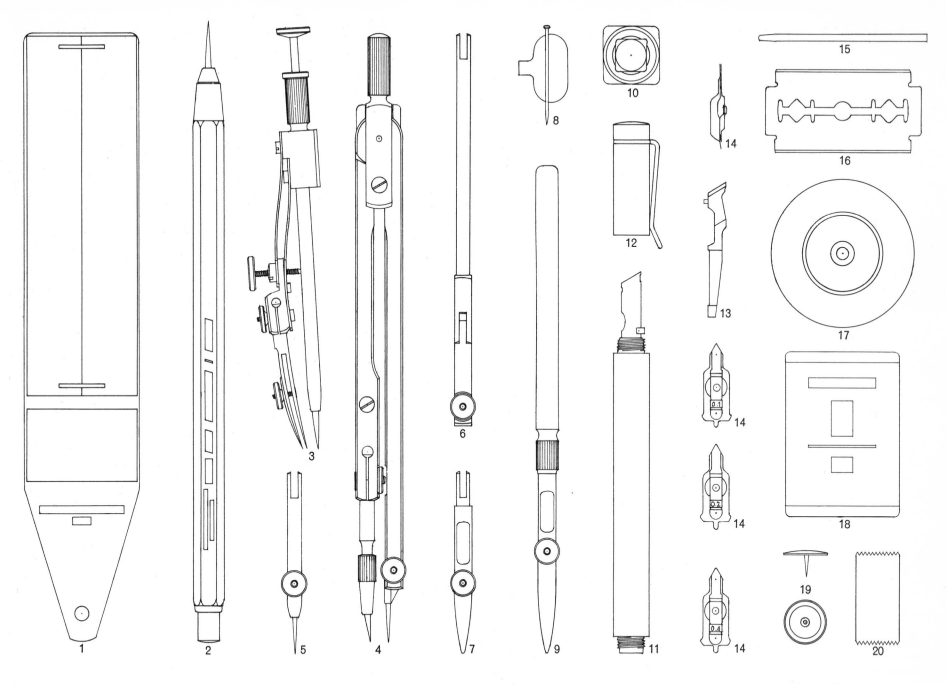

1 Abrasive strip
2 Drawing stylus
3 Spring bow-compasses with drawing pen
4 Compasses with lead insert
5 Divider point for 4

6 Extension for 4
7 Drawing pen for 4
8 Screw tightener and pin
9 Drawing pen with fixed handle
10 Indian-ink cartridge, from above

11 'Graphos' drawing pen
12 Cap for 11
13 Insert for 11
14 Nibs for 11: O 0.2, A 0.1 (0.16), A 0.2 (0.25), A 0.4
15 Matchstick without its head

16 Razor blade
17 Typewriter rubber
18 Erasure mask
19 Drawing pins
20 Adhesive tape

11

Simple working with T-square and set-square

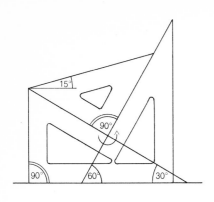

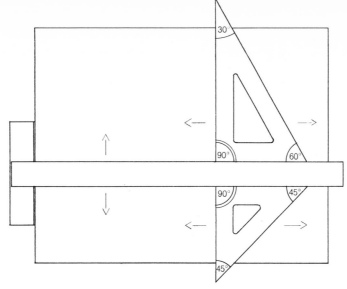

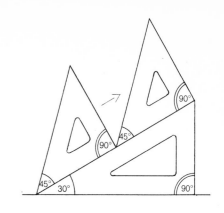

Drawing the normal angles, perpendiculars using the set-square, and the angle 15° by a combination of two set-squares.

Drawing horizontals by T-square, the normal angles and perpendiculars by T-square and set-squares. Keep the head of the T-square firmly against the drawing-board.

Drawing parallels by moving one set-square along another, normal angles, 75° by a combination of set-squares.

Simple working with ruler and compasses

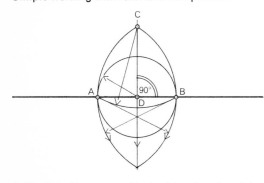

1. To draw the perpendicular bisector of an interval AB.
2. To draw a perpendicular from a point C on to a straight line.
3. To erect a perpendicular at a point D on a straight line.

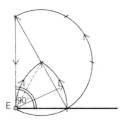

To erect a perpendicular at the end-point of an interval.

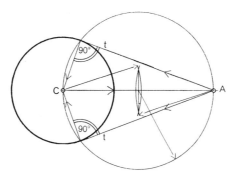

To find the exact points of contact of the tangents t drawn from a given point A to a given circle.

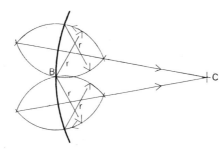

To find the centre of a given circular arc, starting from any point B of the arc.

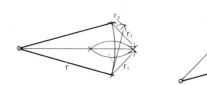

To draw a line through P parallel to a given line.

Bisection and duplication of a given angle.
The radii r and r_1 are arbitrary, r_2 is determined by the given angle

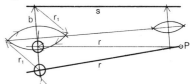

Bisection of an angle with an inaccessible vertex.
The bisector is parallel to the bisector of the vertex angle of the isosceles triangle with sides r, r, which is constructed by drawing a line through P parallel to the upper given line s, and then cutting off the equal lengths r. The third side of this isosceles triangle yields the interval marked b between the given lines. The required bisector is the perpendicular bisector of b.

12

Regular subdivision of a circle

1. Exact constructions

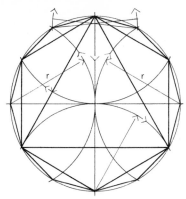

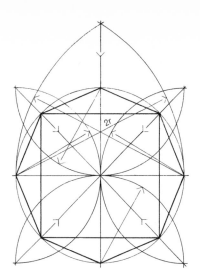

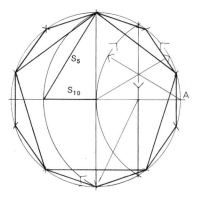

Subdivision into 3, 6 and 12 parts, by successive arcs with the radius r.
Subdivision into 60 parts, as for a clock dial, can be achieved by combining the constructions for 12 parts and 5 parts.

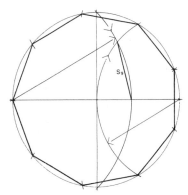

Subdivision into 2, 4 and 8 parts. Simple but important.

A regular octagon drawn in a square.

Subdivision into 5 and 10 parts. This is related to the 'golden section'.
A = initial point;
s_5 = side of pentagon;
s_{10} = side of decagon.

2. Approximate constructions

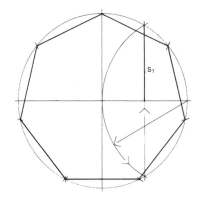

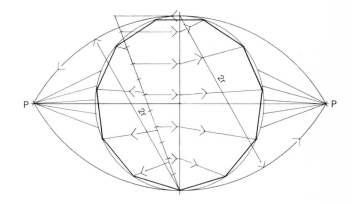

Subdivision into 7 parts
s_7 = side of heptagon
By calculation the error of this construction amounts to $r/2000$.

Subdivision into 9 parts.
s_9 = side of nonagon.
Check by the subdivision into 3 parts.

Subdivision into 11, 13 parts, etc.
Subdivide the diameter into the required number of parts (as shown on page 12, to left). Draw the rays from the poles P through every second point of subdivision along the diameter.

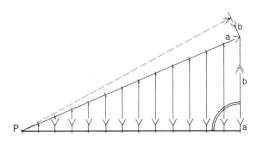

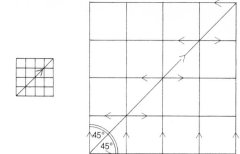

Subdivision of a given interval into a required number of equal parts, say 13. Either draw a line in an arbitrary direction through the end-point of the interval, mark off along it 13 equal intervals on any scale, and transfer the points of subdivision on to the given intervals by lines parallel to the join of the end-points; or, if it is desired to transfer the points of subdivision by lines parallel to a particular direction, say perpendicular to the given interval, we first erect the perpendicular at one end of the given interval, and then rotate a scale about the other end of the interval until 13 of its divisions are cut off between the end-point and the erected perpendicular.

Change of grid
Over a complicated figure a grid of rectangular lines is drawn; the grid is re-drawn on a larger or smaller scale as desired, and points of the figure are plotted on to the new grid.
Enlargement or reduction may be also carried out mechanically using a pantograph. Photographic methods or epidiascopes may also be used.

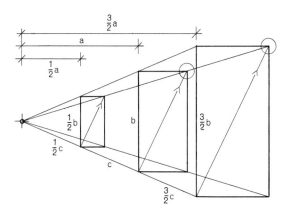

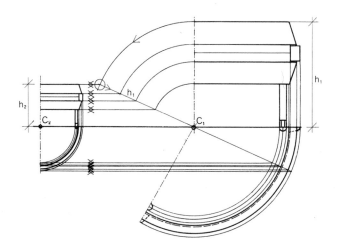

Change of size by ray construction
A figure projected on rays from a point becomes larger or smaller the greater or smaller its distance from the point of projection. The parallel diagonals make accurate drawing easier.

Change of size of solids of revolution by means of circular arcs
In the figure, h_1 and h_2 and either the smaller or larger plan are given.
The plan and elevation of the object—here it is a radio cabinet with a rotatable scale—can be changed in size by drawing a sloping line through the centre C_1 to the point where the horizontal h_2 is cut by the arc of radius h_1. Then all the heights in the right-hand picture can be reduced to the appropriate heights for the left-hand picture, or vice versa.

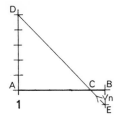

1

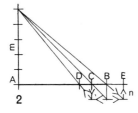

2

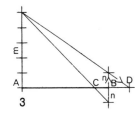

3

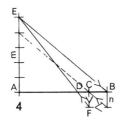

4

1. Division of an interval AB in a given ratio $m : n$ by the join DE of the parallels AD and BE of lengths m and n respectively.

Here AC : CB $= m : n = 5 : 1$

2. Successive reductions or extensions of an interval AB divided in the ratio $m : n$.

AC : CB $=$ AD : DC $=$ AB : BE $= m : n$.

3. Harmonic extension of an interval AB divided in the ratio $m : n = 5 : 1$.

AC : CB $=$ AD : BD $= m : n$.

4. Formation of a harmonic range on a given interval AB with a given ratio $m : n$ ($= 5 : 1$), i.e. to find points C, D such that AB : BC $=$ AD : DC.

Draw the parallels to BE, AE, AB, and the ray EF as shown.

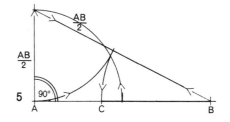

5

5. Division of a given interval AB in the 'Golden Section'. Construction as shown.

AC : BC $=$ BC : AB $= \dfrac{\sqrt{5}-1}{2} \approx 1.618 = k$, say.

AB : BC $= \dfrac{\sqrt{5}-3}{2} \approx 0.618 = q = \dfrac{1}{k}$

6. Extension of a given interval AB to form a Golden Section.

AC : BC $=$ BC : AB $=$ AB : AD.

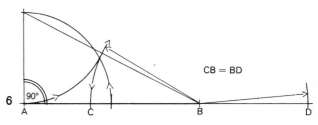

6

7. Representation of the 3 : 4 : 5 right-angled triangle, the 'building triangle', the 'Canon' or alleged Pythagorean basis of the classical and the English units of measurement. Basis 1 foot (30 or 32 cm.).

120	150	180	4	5	6
60	75	90	2	2.5	3
30	37.5	45, etc.	1	1.25	1.5, etc.

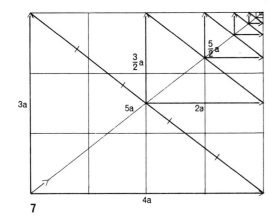

7

8. Representation of Le Corbusier's 'modulor', a subdivision of the Golden Section of Eudoxos of Cnidos. Basis, the 'ideal height of a man' $= 6$ ft $= 1.829$ m.

The factors of $k = 1.618 = 1.309 \times 1.236$

and of $q = \dfrac{1}{k} = 0.618 = 0.809 \times 0.764$

The red series				The blue series
182.9	$\times 1.236$		$=$	226.0
	: 1.309		$=$	139.7
113.0	: 1.309		$=$	86.3
69.8				
$r \cdot q^n$				$b \cdot q^n$

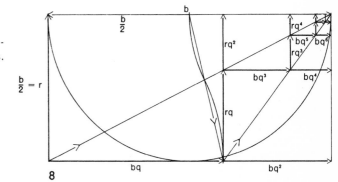

8

Composite curves

I. Composite ovals constructed by circular arcs

The semi-axes a and b are given.

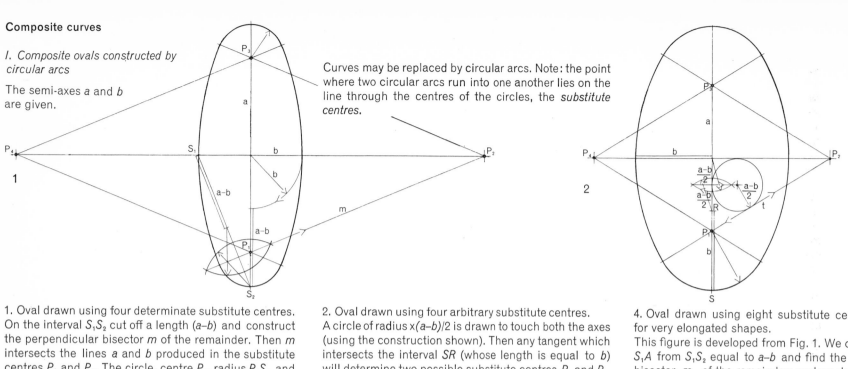

Curves may be replaced by circular arcs. Note: the point where two circular arcs run into one another lies on the line through the centres of the circles, the *substitute centres.*

1. Oval drawn using four determinate substitute centres. On the interval S_1S_2 cut off a length $(a{-}b)$ and construct the perpendicular bisector m of the remainder. Then m intersects the lines a and b produced in the substitute centres P_1 and P_2. The circle, centre P_1, radius P_1S_2, and the circle, centre P_2, radius P_2S_1, of the composite run into one another on the line m. The substitute centres P_3 and P_4 and the rest of the oval is obtained by symmetry.

2. Oval drawn using four arbitrary substitute centres. A circle of radius $\mathrm{x}(a{-}b)/2$ is drawn to touch both the axes (using the construction shown). Then any tangent which intersects the interval SR (whose length is equal to b) will determine two possible substitute centres P_1 and P_2. P_3 and P_4 are obtained by symmetry.

3. Oval drawn using eight substitute centres; suitable for ratios of axes of up to 1 : 2.4. A circle of radius $a{-}b$ is drawn with centre at the point of intersection of the axes. A square is drawn circumscribing this circle, with its vertices on the axes. The distance, c, of the vertices from the centre is doubled to obtain the substitute centres P_3 and P_7 on the minor axis. The eight points labelled P_1 to P_8 in Fig. 3 are the required substitute centres. Starting from P_1 the requisite circular arcs can be drawn to form the composite oval; the arcs with centres P_2 and P_3, for example, run into one another on the line g.

4. Oval drawn using eight substitute centres; suitable for very elongated shapes. This figure is developed from Fig. 1. We cut off a length S_1A from S_1S_2 equal to $a{-}b$ and find the perpendicular bisector, m_1, of the remainder; and we drop a perpendicular from the rectangle corner E on to S_1S_2. The line midway between this perpendicular and m_1 determines the points P_1 and P_2. The line g is drawn through P_2 and A; g determines the end-point R_1 of the circular arc, centre P_2, which goes through S_1. A length R_1R_2 equal to P_1S_2 is now cut off along g to obtain the point R_2. The perpendicular bisector, m_2, of the interval R_2P_1 cuts g in the substitute centre P_3. The remaining substitute centres can be obtained by symmetry.

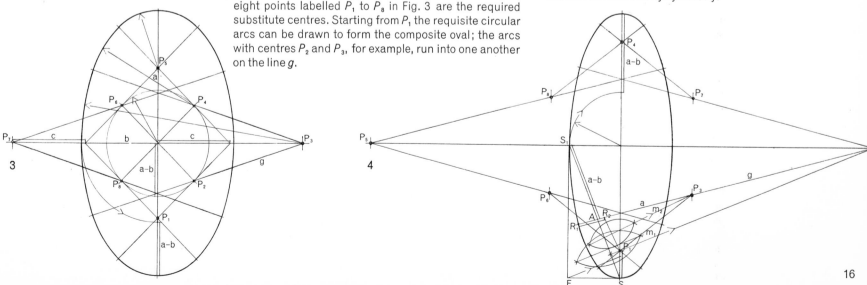

16

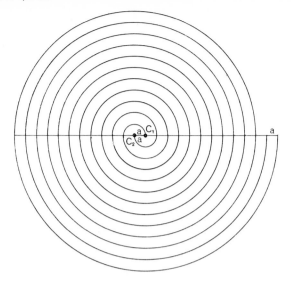

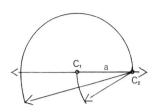

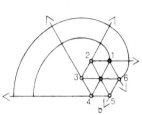

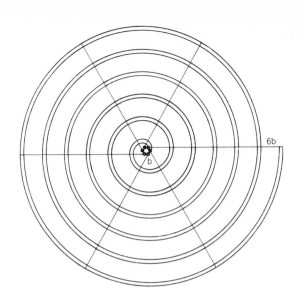

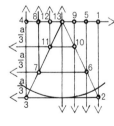

1. The simplest double spiral is constructed from successive semicircles increasing in radius by 2*a* after each revolution. The circular arcs are drawn about the centres C_1 and C_2 with radii *a*, 2*a*, 3*a*..., where $C_1C_2 = a$.

2. A periodic regular double spiral is constructed from circular arcs subtending 60° at their centres. After each revolution the radius increases by 6*b*, which is the length of the periphery of the hexagonal kernel. Arcs are drawn with radius *b* round points 1 and 2, radius 2*b* round points 2 and 3, 3*b* round points 3 and 4, and so on.

3. Spiral drawn with the kernel 0, *a*/3, 2*a*/3, 3*a*/3, which increases arithmetically. The spiral fits in rectangles of 12×14 and 14×16 squares of side *a*. It consists of successive quarter-circles drawn about the points (1), 2, 3 of the kernel. The arc drawn round the point 13 has radius equal to *a*.

4. Spiral drawn with the kernel 0, *b*/4, *b*/2, *b*, which increases geometrically. The spiral fits in rectangles of 10×12 and 12×14 squares of side *b*. It consists of successive quarter-circles drawn about the points (1), 2, 3. The arc drawn round the point 13 has radius equal to *b*.

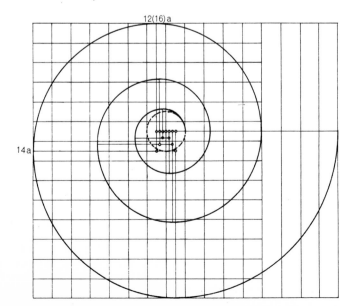

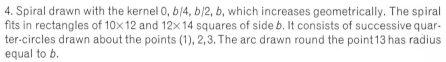

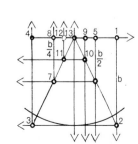

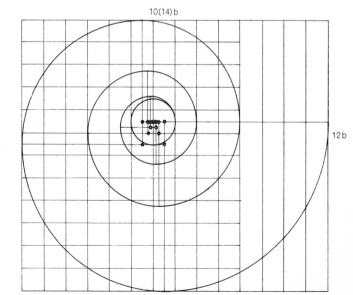

Construction of an Ellipse

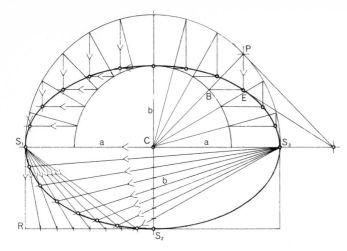

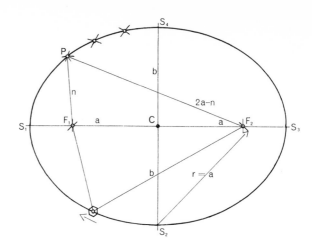

Construction by rays, the principal axes 2a, 2b being given.
1. Circles are drawn with centre C, radii a and b. If a radius cuts the outer circle in P and the inner circle in B, a line through P parallel to b and a line through B parallel to a will intersect in a point E of the required ellipse.
2. The intervals S_2C and S_2R are divided into the same number of equal parts. Corresponding rays from S_1 to successive points of subdivision of S_2R (starting from S_2) and from S_3 to the points of subdivision of S_2IC (starting from S_2) will intercept in points of the ellipse.

Construction by means of a thread or circular arcs, the principal axes 2a and 2b being given.
A circle, centre S_2, radius a, determines the foci F_1, F_2 on S_1S_3. If a string of length $2a$ is attached to pins at F_1 and F_2, a pencil point held in the loop will trace out the ellipse. Alternatively, points of the ellipse can be obtained as the points of intersection of circular arcs, one centred at F_1 with radius n say, the other centred at F_2 with radius $2a–n$, so that the sum of the radii is always equal to $2a$.

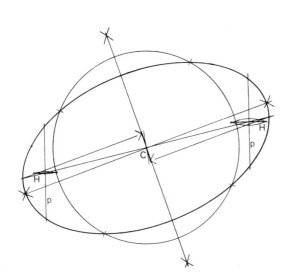

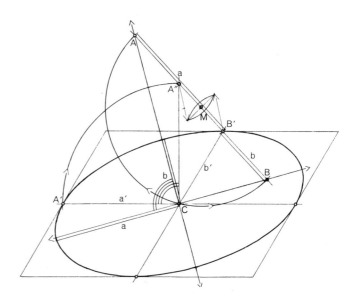

Determination of the principal axes of an ellipse (already drawn).
Draw two parallel chords p of the ellipse. Determine the mid-points H of the chords p and draw a third chord through these mid-points. Find the mid-point C of this third chord, and draw a circle round C to intersect the ellipse in four points. Then the perpendicular bisectors of the joins of adjacent points of intersection are the principal axes.

Determination of the principal axes of an ellipse from a given pair of conjugate diameters a′ and b′.
Rotate the point A' through 90° round C to A'', draw a line through A'', B', and determine the mid-point M of $A''B'$. A circle, centre M, radius MC determines the points A and B on the line $A''B'$. Then CA and CB are the directions of the principal axes; moreover, the lengths $B'A = a$ and $B'B = b$ are the lengths of the principal semi-axes.

18

Construction of a Parabola

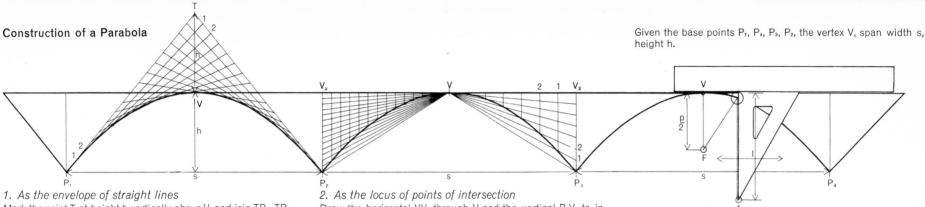

1. As the envelope of straight lines
Mark the point T at height h vertically above V, and join TP_1, TP_2. Divide TP_1 and TP_2 into an equal number of parts, and join the points of subdivision starting from the bottom on P_1 T and from the top on TP_2 as shown. The parabola is the envelope of the successive line segments.

2. As the locus of points of intersection
Draw the horizontal VV_3 through V and the vertical P_3V_3 to intersect in V_3. Divide VV_3 and P_3V_3 into n equal parts, labelling the points of subdivision from V_2 and from P_2 respectively. Then the verticals through the points 1, 2, ... on the horizontal intersect the rays from V to the points 1, 2, ... on the vertical respectively in points of the parabola.

3. By means of string, pin, T-square and set-square
A pin is stuck in at the focus F situated at a distance p/2 below V, where $p/2 = s^2/16h$. The T-square and set-square are arranged as shown. A string of length l + p/2 is fastened to the pin at F and to the point A of the set-square, l being the length of the side of the set-square. As the set-square is moved along the T-square, a pencil point inserted in the string and held close to the side of the set-square will trace out the parabola.

Construction of a Hyperbola

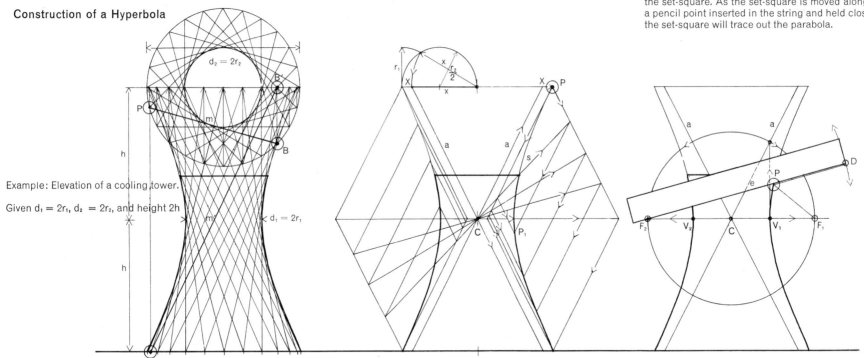

Example: Elevation of a cooling tower.

Given $d_1 = 2r_1$, $d_2 = 2r_2$, and height 2h.

1. As the envelope of straight lines
Vertically above the elevation, the plan is drawn, consisting of two concentric circles of radii r_1 and r_2. Arbitrary generators such as m are drawn, touching the inner circle and intersecting the outer circle in the points P and B. If P is projected vertically to P' on the base line of the elevation, and B is projected to B' on the top line of the elevation, then the various lines such as P'B' will envelop the required hyperbola.

2. As the locus of points of intersection
First we plot the points X whose coordinates are, relative to the centre C: h above C, and $x = \sqrt{r_2^2 - r_1^2}$ horizontally to the side of C. A geometrical construction for the points X is indicated at the top left of the diagram.
Through the centre C and the two points X the lines marked a are drawn. To draw the hyperbola through the point P, we first draw parallels through P to the two lines a. At the points where any ray such as s from C intersects these two lines we complete the parallelogram; the vertex P of this parallelogram is a new point on the hyperbola. By choosing various rays s we obtain as many points as we need to draw the hyperbola.

3. By means of string and a strip of cardboard
The lines a are drawn first as in method 2. At the vertex V a perpendicular is erected, and this determines a length e along one of the lines a. Then a circle with centre C and radius e determines the foci F_1 and F_2 on the horizontal through C. A strip of cardboard is fastened so that it can rotate about F_2. A string of length $F_2D - F_2V_1 + V_1F_1 = DPF_1$ is fastened to F_1 and the cardboard at D. Then a pencil point inserted in the string and held close to the side of the cardboard strip will trace out the required hyperbola as the strip is rotated. The other branch of the hyperbola can be obtained similarly or can be drawn as the mirror image of the first branch in the vertical through C.

An illustration of the use of the construction given on page 16

The Vienna Stadium (Architect: O. E. Schweizer)
Plane, scale 1:1250.
The replacement of mathematical curves by composite
curves made up of circular arcs or straight-line intervals
is, of course, inaccurate, but in certain circumstances it
may have considerable practical advantages.

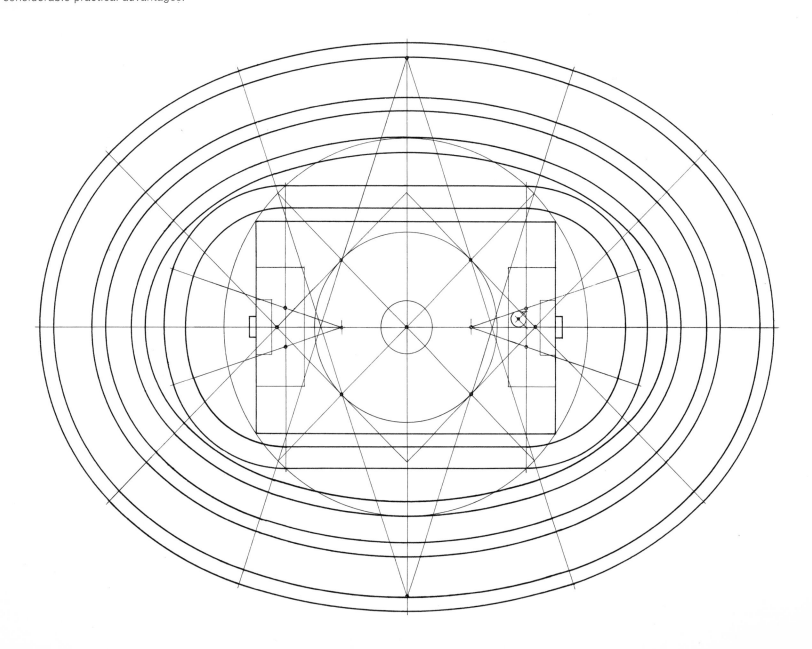

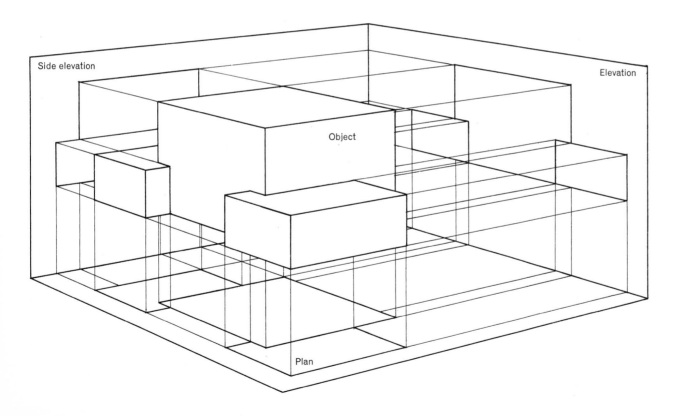

Side elevation

Elevation

Object

Plan

In engineering drawings we lay down the shape and arrangement, the dimensions and materials, of things to be manufactured; we preserve information in this form about things in existence or even about those which have ceased to exist.

All the details of the solid object to be represented are projected by parallel, rectilinear rays on to suitably placed planes to obtain 'plans', i. e. plane drawings of the three-dimensional object. The picture which is produced by projecting all details of the object vertically downwards on to the horizontal plane is called the *plan*. The plan will therefore contain the dimensions of all lengths and breadths but no heights.

The *elevation* and the *side elevation* are similarly obtained by parallel projection on to vertical planes. The elevation gives the front view and therefore includes the dimensions for heights and widths but no lengths (depths); the side elevation gives the side view and shows heights and lengths (depths) accurately, but contains no widths. We may also imagine the plan, elevation, and side elevation as representing the intersections of other horizontal and vertical planes with the object; it may be desirable to represent the intersections by several successive horizontal planes, say, separately, since to put these all on top of one another would be too confusing.

Engineering drawings must be of a handy size, enabling the whole drawing to be seen at once, and so the plans etc. are usually considerably reduced in size, e. g. in the ratios 1:1000, 1:500, 1:200, 1:100, 1:50, 1:20, 1:10. Half-scale drawings should be avoided, since they can easily lead to errors in reading off dimensions. This reduction of scale will often entail a certain simplification; many details may only be shown in outline or be indicated by conventional signs.

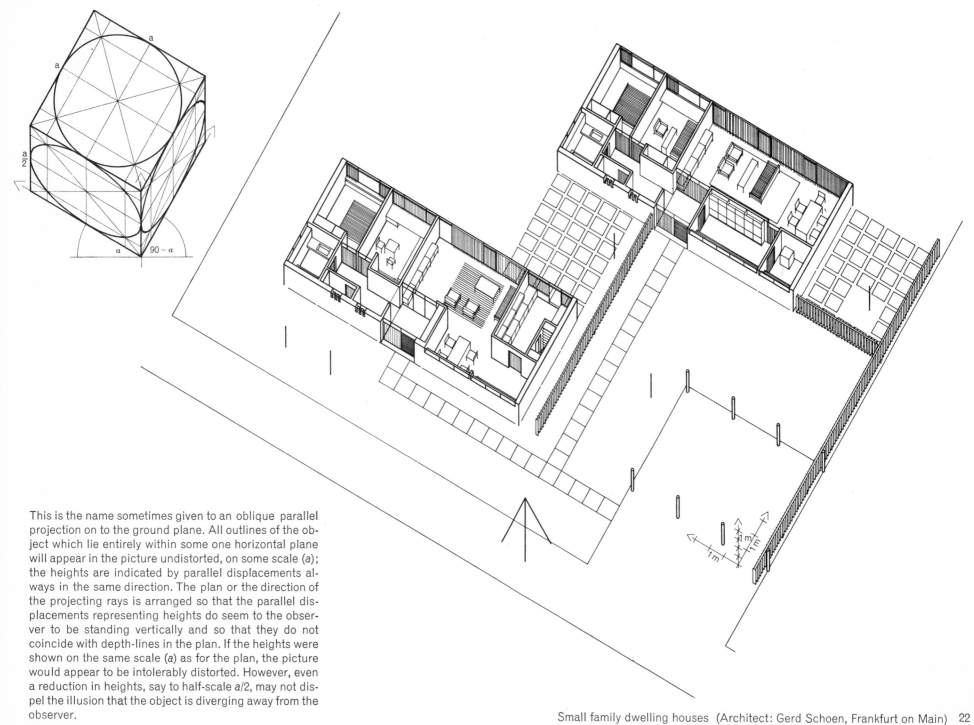

This is the name sometimes given to an oblique parallel projection on to the ground plane. All outlines of the object which lie entirely within some one horizontal plane will appear in the picture undistorted, on some scale (*a*); the heights are indicated by parallel displacements always in the same direction. The plan or the direction of the projecting rays is arranged so that the parallel displacements representing heights do seem to the observer to be standing vertically and so that they do not coincide with depth-lines in the plan. If the heights were shown on the same scale (*a*) as for the plan, the picture would appear to be intolerably distorted. However, even a reduction in heights, say to half-scale *a*/2, may not dispel the illusion that the object is diverging away from the observer.

Small family dwelling houses (Architect: Gerd Schoen, Frankfurt on Main) 22

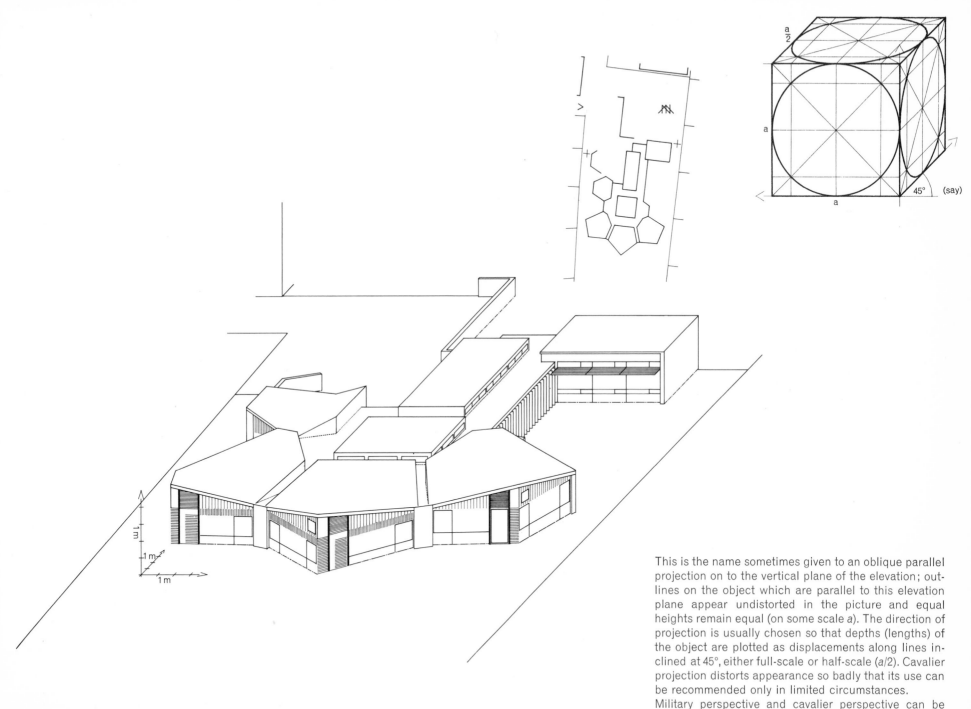

This is the name sometimes given to an oblique parallel projection on to the vertical plane of the elevation; outlines on the object which are parallel to this elevation plane appear undistorted in the picture and equal heights remain equal (on some scale *a*). The direction of projection is usually chosen so that depths (lengths) of the object are plotted as displacements along lines inclined at 45°, either full-scale or half-scale (*a*/2). Cavalier projection distorts appearance so badly that its use can be recommended only in limited circumstances.

Military perspective and cavalier perspective can be drawn without knowing anything about the true principles of perspective.

23   Kindergarten (Architect: Fritz Zeiger VfA, Cologne)

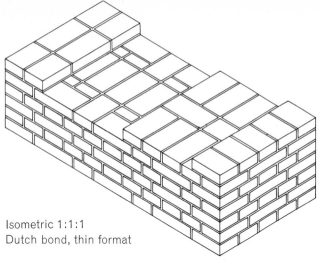

Isometric 1:1:1
Dutch bond, thin format

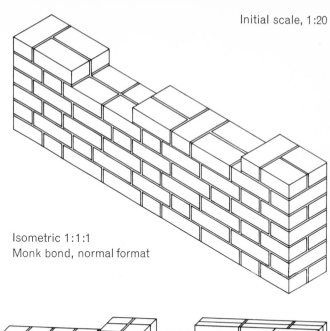

Isometric 1:1:1
Monk bond, normal format

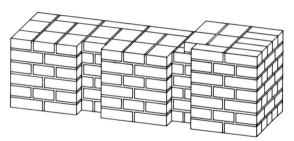

Dimetric 1:1: $^1/_3$
English cross bond, thin format

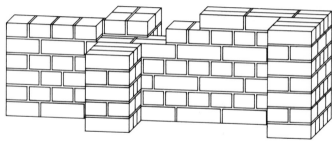

Dimetric 1:1: $^1/_4$
English cross bond, normal format

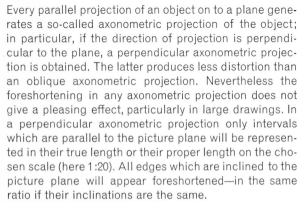

Every parallel projection of an object on to a plane generates a so-called axonometric projection of the object; in particular, if the direction of projection is perpendicular to the plane, a perpendicular axonometric projection is obtained. The latter produces less distortion than an oblique axonometric projection. Nevertheless the foreshortening in any axonometric projection does not give a pleasing effect, particularly in large drawings. In a perpendicular axonometric projection only intervals which are parallel to the picture plane will be represented in their true length or their proper length on the chosen scale (here 1:20). All edges which are inclined to the picture plane will appear foreshortened—in the same ratio if their inclinations are the same.

In order to be able to read off heights and widths on the desired scales, therefore, we start from objects of increased size. Lines which are parallel to the picture plane, e. g. one particular diameter of a sphere or circle,

will therefore appear enlarged. The direction of projection can be arranged so that the units of length for the (foreshortened) heights, widths, and depths bear simple ratios to one another; for example, if they are equal, 1:1:1, the projection is *isometric*; if they are 1:1:$^1/_2$, the projection is a *dimetric* one, the essential feature of a dimetric projection being that two scales are needed for dimensioning the drawing. A *trimetric* projection requires three different scales for heights, widths, and depths. By choosing simple numerical ratios the drawing of isometric, dimetric, or even trimetric projections is made quite easy.

The following ratios are commonly used.

	D : B : H	a : b	c : d	g	k
Isometric 1:1:1		tan 30°	tan 30°	$\frac{\sqrt{6}}{2}=1.2247$	$\frac{\sqrt{2}}{2}=0.707$
Dimetric $^1/_2$:1:1		~ 7:8	~ 1:8	$\frac{3\sqrt{2}}{4}=1.0607$	$k_1=\frac{\sqrt{2}}{4}=0.3535$
					$k_2=\frac{\sqrt{14}}{4}=0,935$
Dimetric $^1/_3$:1:1		~ 17:18	~ 1:18	1.0275	
Dimetric $^1/_4$:1:1		~ 31:32	~ 1:32	1.0155	
Trimetric $^2/_3$:$^5/_6$:1		~ 1:3	~ 1:5	1.0342	
Trimetric $^1/_2$:$^9/_{10}$:1		~ 1:3	~ 1:11	1.0148	

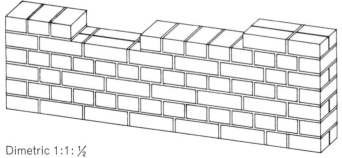

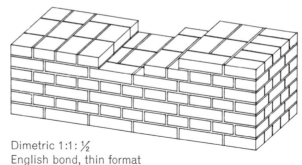

Dimetric 1:1: ½
English cross bond, normal format

Dimetric 1:1: ½
English bond, thin format

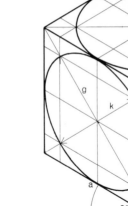

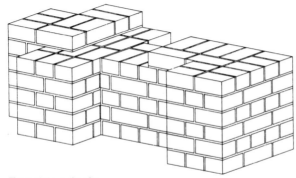

Trimetric 1:²/₃:⁵/₆
English bond, normal format

Trimetric 1:½:⁹/₁₀
English bond, thin format

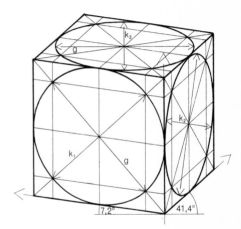

D   unit of length for depths
B   unit of length for breadths
H   unit of length for heights
a:b and c:d   slope of the axes for breadths and depths relative to the picture plane
g   length of the maximum diameter of a sphere, parallel to the picture plane
k   length of the minimum diameter, perpendicular to g.

Method
Object heights are plotted vertically and to their proper size (on the initially chosen scale), breadths are plotted in a given direction to the one side, and depths along a second given direction to the other side. Dimensions can be plotted or taken off only parallel to the three principal directions, of course.

The simplest axonometric perpendicular projection—the isometric projection, in which heights, breadths, and depths are plotted on the same scale—looks particularly awkward, and for symmetric objects is rather unrepresentative because the front and back edges appear to be collinear. The axonometric projection most commonly employed is the dimetric one with heights and breadths plotted to the same scale, and depths to half-scale.
In an isometric projection a given circle, irrespective of which face of a represented cube it may lie on, will have the same elliptic image, though with different orientations. In a dimetric projection, the same circle will have two different elliptic images, and in a trimetric projection three different elliptic images. For drawing the elliptic images of circles in isometric projection or the 1:1:¹/₂ dimetric projection, special stencils are available; these also show the normal angles, and their use is to be recommended.

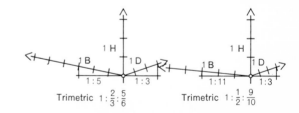

Dimetric 1:1:⅓   Dimetric 1:1:¼

Trimetric 1:²/₃:⁵/₆   Trimetric 1:½:⁹/₁₀

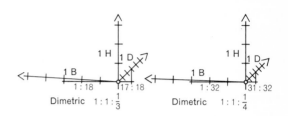

25

The Perspectograph

Light from our environment enters our eye in a wide cone. If we interpose a transparent surface in this cone and mark each point where it is intersected by a ray of light with a spot of the corresponding colour, we obtain a picture exactly like nature—a perspective.

A thoroughly practical instrument embodying this principle is the 'perspectograph'. A home-made version can easily be constructed from two boards or a metal arm, a large ball-and-socket joint, and a rigid tripod stand. A sheet of glass is supported upright on the horizontal arm, and an eyepiece is located centrally relative to the glass, the distance between the two being 50 to 60 cm (19 to 24 in.), depending on the range. A sheet of transparent washable film is attached to the glass plate, and the instrument is directed towards the object to be represented. The observer looks through the eyepiece and simply draws with a wax pencil on the film what he can see of the object with his eye in that fixed position; so the required picture is obtained. The perspectograph must stand rigidly.

If a perspectograph is to be used to fill in details on a perspective which has already been drawn, then the actual standpoint, the direction of the principal visual ray, and the distance between station point and picture plane (these technical terms are defined on pages 27–29) must be exactly the same as they were when the perspective was first drawn; the instrument needs to be exactly calibrated and orientated.

The plane sheet of glass in the perspectograph could be replaced by a piece curved into cylindrical or spherical shape, preferably arranged so that the eyepiece would be situated on the axis of the cylinder or at the centre of the sphere respectively. After the picture had been drawn, the curved glass sheets would have to be viewed from a point corresponding to the original position of the eyepiece. In such cases it would be best to draw directly on to the glass. Almost all the lines of the object would appear as curves on the curved glass surface. This makes no difference in the drawing of the perspective using the perspectograph; but to *construct* a perspective as it would appear on a curved surface entails an enormous amount of work which is hardly ever warranted.

For theatre scene-designers it is of interest that a perspectograph can be fitted with, not one but, a number of glass screens arranged one behind the other; on the furthest one the background may be drawn, and on the others the various sets for the wings, such as plants, houses, and so on. By using several eyepieces we can even take the flooring and the different tiers of seats into account.

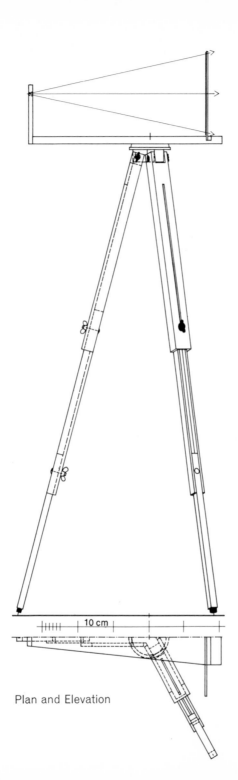

10 cm

Plan and Elevation

Isometric Projection

26

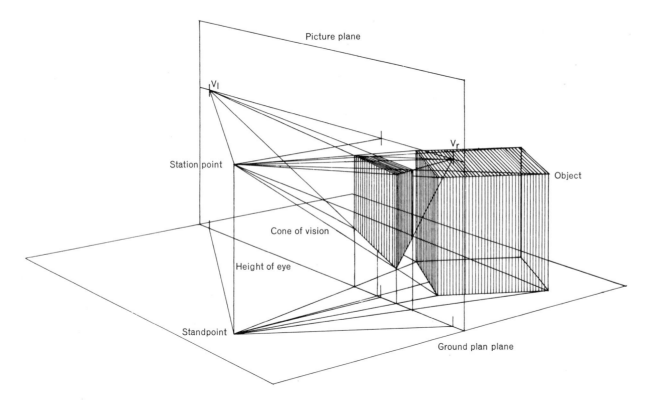

Picture plane

V$_l$

V$_r$

Station point

Object

Cone of vision

Height of eye

Standpoint

Ground plan plane

General Information
A perspective construction depends on:
1. The object. Simple, rectilinear, right-angled, crystalliform bodies are the easiest to represent.
2. The station point, i. e. the position of the eye viewing the object. This position is the decisive factor governing the appearance of the perspective drawing; it should be chosen so that the angle of vision is 30°–45°, it is for the picture and should also be in fact the best point of observation.
3. The picture plane. This is best vertical and perpendicular to the cone of vision. Its distance from the station point determines the size of the picture, and its position relative to the object determines the accuracy of the representation. The differences of the perspective drawing from what is actually seen arise because the picture plane is a *plane*.
4. The cone of vision. The picture may be regarded as the totality of the points of intersection of the rays from the object to the station point with the picture plane.

1. The object

The flatter, more rectilinear, more simply right-angled, more symmetric, and the more crystalliform or periodically repetitive an object is, the easier it is to represent it in perspective; the more it takes on an organic or living, a random or free form, the harder it is so to represent it. The difficulty increases the more irregular the object is and to such an extent that, with objects like trees, plants or rocks, for example, we have to limit ourselves to the essential features, outline patterns, the axes and principal masses. This is because it is essential to know exactly the ground plan and elevation of an object in order to make a perspective drawing of it.

2. The station point

To produce the illusion of three-dimensionality it is important and not at all easy to find the proper standpoint and the proper height of eye vertically above it for the station point. The direction of the cone of vision, i. e. the pencil of rays from the station point which envelop the object, gives the perspective its name and character. If this cone is directed vertically upwards from the station point, we have a 'ceiling perspective'; if it is directed vertically downwards, we have a 'ground perspective'. A downward perspective is called a 'bird's-eye view'; an upward perspective is called a 'worm's-eye view'. Their effect can best be appreciated by examining pictures or architectural photographs.

The 'worm's-eye view' was first widely used in 1451 by Andrea Mantegna in the Ovetari Chapel of St. Agostino degli Eremitani in Padua. The frescoes there begin above the height of eye of the faithful, for whom they were drawn; so floors are nowhere to be seen in them, we look from below at men, houses, and arches, all towering upwards. The figures appear to pass by above the observer or even to be about to tread on him and so compel his attention. Bird's-eye views have been painted by scarcely any painter more frequently than by Pieter Brueghel. The spectator has the impression of floating above the proceedings and seeing everything.

So far as possible only those station points and directions of vision should be adopted which the observer would customarily have if the object had been completed. Since, when looking at pictures, we do not approach closer than reading-distance, the distance from the station point to the picture plane should not be less than 12 inches.

The difference between what we actually see and a perspective drawing often leads us to feel that the latter is distorted. The perspective is drawn from one point and for just one point, the station point. But our vision is

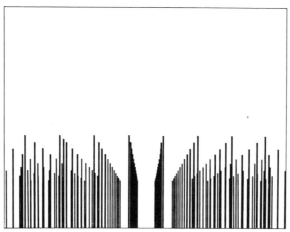

Worm's-eye view

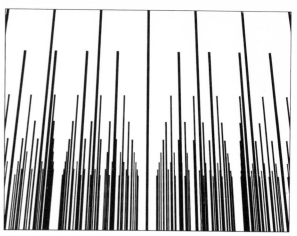

Worm's-eye view with toppling verticals

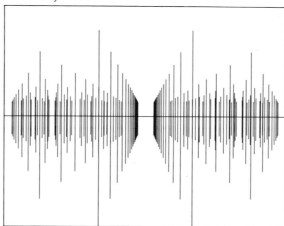

Normal perspective

Ground perspective

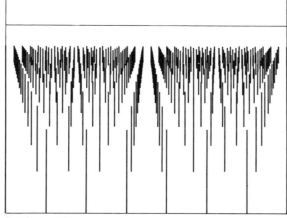

Bird's-eye view

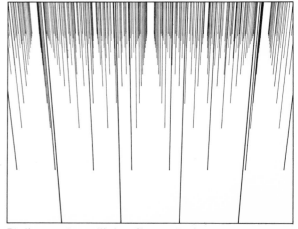

Bird's-eye view with toppling verticals

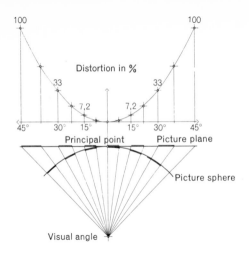

Distortion diagram.
The deviation from the principal ray determines the distortion in the picture.

binocular. The larger the picture in comparison with the interocular distance, the more closely the perspective drawing represents what we actually see. If we could compel an observer to close one eye and to take up the original station point, which is also the ideal position for observing the picture, he would then be situated at a point where the picture subtends an angle of 90° or even more.

Viewed from any other position, the details would be all the more distorted the greater their distance on the picture plane from the principal point, i. e. the point where the principal (perpendicular) ray from the station point cuts the picture plane. The distortion varies with the square of the angular deviation from the direction of the principal ray; the distortion is equal to

100%   or $^1/_1$ at 45°
33.3%   or $^1/_3$ at 30°
7.2%   or $^1/_{14}$ at 15°

Consequently the angle of vision should be limited to 30° for the object in exterior perspectives (because the empty space also counts towards the picture), and for interiors to 45° or at most 60°, depending on the circumstances. The most important consequence of this restriction on the angle of vision is that the object must not be too closely approached. The necessary distance can easily be found by applying a 30° or 45° setsquare to the plan drawing or to a rough scale model. If more than one corner of a room has to be shown in a perspective drawing of an interior, the station point will, in general, necessarily be outside this room, at a point, in fact, from which

in actuality nothing at all could be seen of the interior. However, the height of eye and the centre of vision, that is, the line along which the observer's eye is supposed to be directed, should at least be chosen so as to be actually possible for an observer entering the room.

3. The picture plane

The picture plane must be arranged so that the axis or bisector of the angle of the cone of vision coincides with the shortest distance, i. e the perpendicular, from the station point to the picture plane; this direction is also called the principal ray. The foot of this perpendicular, the principal point, P, should then lie at about the centre of the picture. However, these rules cannot always be strictly applied; for perspectives which are even only slightly diagonal a horizontal vanishing point becomes inaccessible. In perspectives looking upward or downward the inclination of the picture plane to the horizontal makes the drawing more difficult, and, as in photography, gives rise to toppling verticals: verticals on the object are no longer represented as vertical lines. The distance of the picture plane in front of the station point is determined by the positions of the object and station point and the desired size of picture. For a fixed distance between station point and object, the further the picture plane is placed from the station point, the more the cone of vision expands (and correspondingly, the greater the effect of drawing errors), and hence the greater the area of its intersection with the picture plane; i. e. the bigger the picture, though its proportions do not change. Conversely, the shorter the distance d becomes, that is, the part of the principal ray between the station point and the picture plane, the smaller the picture becomes.

4. The cone of vision

The point of the picture corresponding to a particular point of the object is situated where the ray from the object point to the station point cuts the picture plane. Any part of the object which lies in front of the picture plane will appear magnified in the picture, and anything lying behind the picture plane will appear reduced. Only the part lying in the picture plane will appear on the same scale as the object. It is therefore sensible to make the picture plane intersect the object along any particularly important vertical edge. This edge then forms part of the picture itself and can be plotted into it directly, together with the height of eye, h_e, using the scale of the plan of the object. Outlines on the object which lie in planes parallel to the picture plane will only be magnified or diminished by the projection, but the proportions in each will not be distorted. In particular, straight lines running

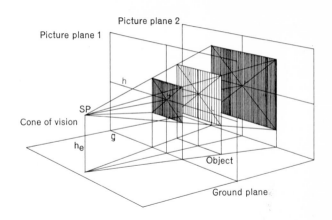

The distance of the picture plane from the station point determines the size of the picture.

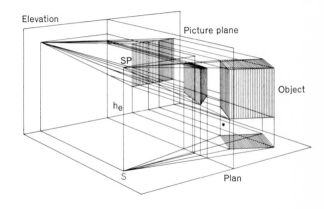

The point where a visual ray to a point of the object cuts the picture plane is the image of that object point.

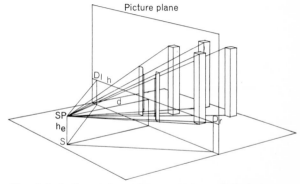

Parallels to the picture plane remain undistorted.

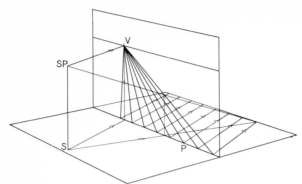

The vanishing point for parallel lines is constructed by means of a parallel to them through the station point or standpoint.

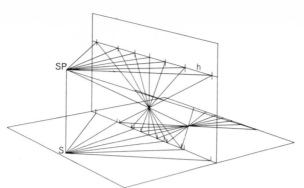

The vanishing points of horizontal lines lie on the horizon.

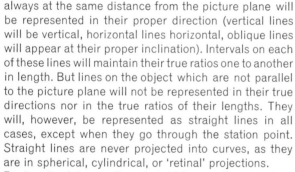

The centre of vision, the vanishing point of the depth lines, lies at the centre of the picture on the horizon. The 'distance points', the vanishing points for the horizontal diagonals, are at a distance d from the centre of vision to the left and right respectively along the horizon line.

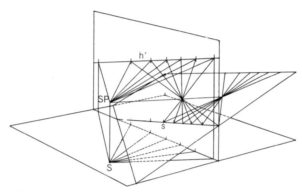

Straight lines in one or several oblique planes also have a 'horizon', namely the vanishing trace h'. The intersections h' and s are parallel.

always at the same distance from the picture plane will be represented in their proper direction (vertical lines will be vertical, horizontal lines horizontal, oblique lines will appear at their proper inclination). Intervals on each of these lines will maintain their true ratios one to another in length. But lines on the object which are not parallel to the picture plane will not be represented in their true directions nor in the true ratios of their lengths. They will, however, be represented as straight lines in all cases, except when they go through the station point. Straight lines are never projected into curves, as they are in spherical, cylindrical, or 'retinal' projections.

For brevity, let us call a straight line on the object an object-line. An object-line which is not parallel to the picture plane, supposed extended indefinitely, must always cut it somewhere; so that *one* image point, P say, for this object-line can certainly be discovered. The image of an object-line is a straight line, and a straight line can

be drawn when two points on it are known; so we need a second image point. Now since the picture plane is often chosen to be in front of the object, between the latter and the observer, the point of intersection of the object-line with the picture plane is the *nearest* point of that line. It follows that the drawing will have the greatest accuracy if we choose as the second point to define the image line the image of the *most distant* point on the object-line. If we look at a line receding into the distance, in the end we are looking in a direction which is, to all intents and purposes, parallel to that line. This means that we can regard the point where the picture plane is cut by a line drawn through the station point parallel to the given object-line as the image of a point on the object-line which is indefinitely far removed. Object-lines which are parallel to one another but not to the picture plane are represented by straight lines which concur in one point, the 'vanishing point' *V*. Each set of parallel object-

lines which are not parallel to the picture plane has its own vanishing point. If, in the perspective, we think only of horizontal visual rays through the station point in various directions, these will cut the picture plane in a line each point of which is at eye-level; this is the 'horizon'. The vanishing points of all horizontal lines all lie on the horizon.

In a normally constructed perspective with a perpendicular picture plane, the centre of vision—which is the vanishing point of all straight lines perpendicular to the picture plane, known as 'depth lines'—is situated *at the centre of the picture on the horizon*. Everything which is situated at eye-level, for example, the heads of people of the same height standing in a large square, or the ears of a field of high standing wheat in a plain, appear on the horizon. The horizon line separates everything on a higher level which is seen from below from everything on a lower level which is seen from above.

Perspective with Visual Rays, Constructed without Vanishing Points

Required: Plan and elevation. Principal ray parallel.
Scale here, 1 : 50

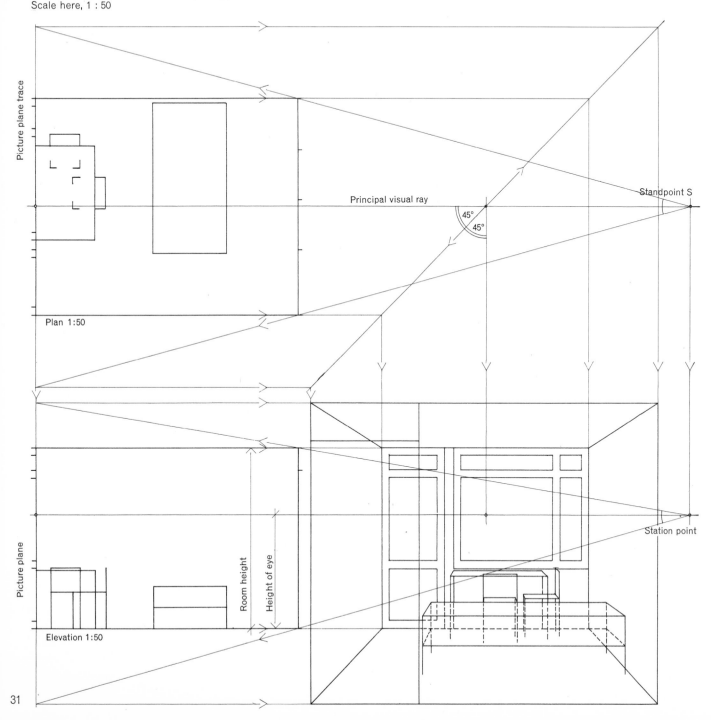

Picture plane trace

Standpoint S

Principal visual ray

45°
45°

Plan 1:50

Picture plane

Room height

Height of eye

Station point

Elevation 1:50

This perspective, in which visual rays in the plan and elevation determine the width and height of the picture, is of general application and is easily understood. Since, however, it does not admit of any possible simplifications and checks, it is seldom used in its pure form; it is mainly used for the representation of very complicated objects, such as spiral staircases, for instance.

The principal visual ray in the ground plan is drawn parallel to the long edge of the drawing-board about a quarter way from the top of the board; on it is the plan (drawn here to the scale 1:50) and the standpoint S. S is placed so that everything which it is desired to represent is seen within an angle of about 30°. The picture plane, which appears here only as a straight line, called the picture plane trace, is drawn perpendicular to the principal visual ray and at the appropriate distance from S to give the desired width of the picture. The plan positions of all objects are projected on to the picture plane by visual rays.

Vertically below the plan drawing an elevation is drawn to the same scale on a line parallel to the principal visual ray in the plan; this line represents the ground plane and it may be drawn at any convenient level. Of course, if the elevation is already available, it can be simply fastened to the board vertically below the plan. Eye-level is marked off in the elevation drawing, and the station point and picture plane are obtained by drawing verticals from the corresponding positions in the upper part of the diagram. Visual rays from the station point to the various object points give the height at the picture plane of the required image points. These heights will be transferred horizontally using the T-square.

A vertical central axis is chosen for the desired picture, and through its intersection with the principal visual ray in the plan drawing a line is drawn at inclination 45°. Widths in the upper (plan) drawing are transferred horizontally to the 45° line and then vertically downward. The intersection of each of these vertical lines with the appropriate height lines gives the image points. On joining corresponding image points the perspective drawing is obtained.

The transfer of the widths from the plan—where they are measured vertically—to the picture can also be carried out, either separately by dividers or all together using a marked paper strip; these widths being laid off from the central vertical axis of the picture.

Provided that the plan and elevation represent one and the same situation seen from above and from the side, the drawings in plan and elevation need not necessarily be arranged as just described; see the perspectives on pages 104 and 105.

Central Perspective with Plan

Required: Plan and elevation. Scale here, 1:50

1 Plan, standpoint, picture plane

Room	4.20×5.00 m. 2.40 m. high
	(14 ft. × 16 ft. 6 in. 8 ft. high)
Dining table	1.20×0.80 m. 0.76 m. high (4 ft.× 31 in.
	30 in. high)
Chairs	0.40×0.40 m. 0.47 m. high, backs 0.76 m.
	(16 in.× 16 in.
	19 in. high, backs 30 in.)
Armchairs	0.60×0.60 m. 0.18, 0.36, 0.60 m. high
	(24 in.× 24 in.
	7 in., 14 in., 24 in. high)
Settee	1.80×0.75 m. 0.18, 0.36, 0.60 m. high
	(6 ft. × 30 in.
	7 in., 14 in. 24 in. high)
Occasional	0.90×0.60 m. 0.48 m. high
table	(3 ft × 24 in. 19 in. high)
Bookcases	0.70×0.35 m. 0.06, 0.30, 0.60 m. high
	(28 in.× 14 in. 2¹/₂ in., 12 in., 24 in. high)

The plan is fixed parallel to the edge of the drawing-board. The standpoint S is arranged centrally in front of it so that the angle of vision which will include all that is to be shown amounts to about 30°–40° (for interior spaces, up to about 60°). The picture plane PP is drawn perpendicular to the bisector of the angle of vision, the principal visual ray, and at an arbitrary distance from the standpoint; preferred positions are in the nearer or further walls of the room. The picture arises as the totality of the points of intersection with the picture plane of the visual rays between object and standpoint. A picture plane between the standpoint and the plan gives a smaller, more accurate picture, a picture plane beyond the plan gives a larger, less accurate picture.

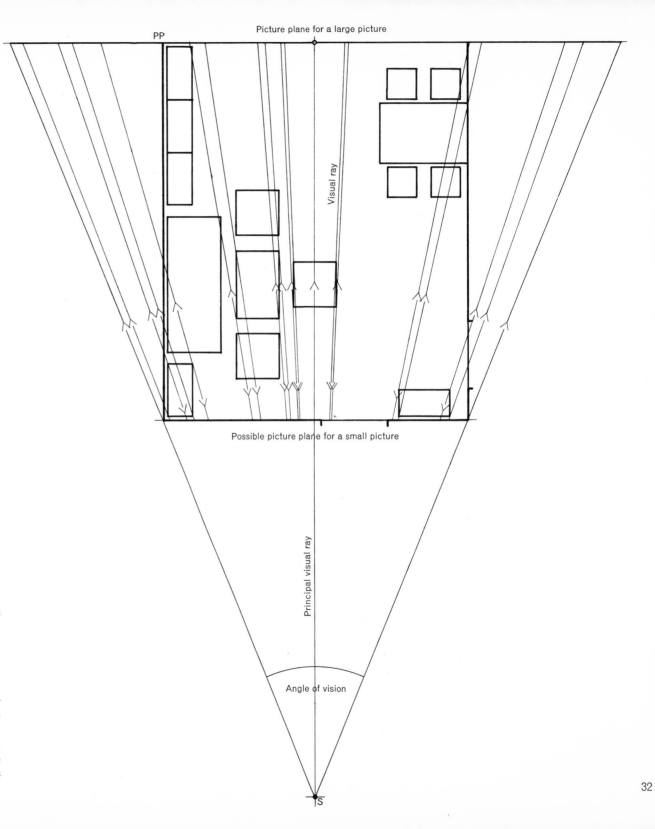

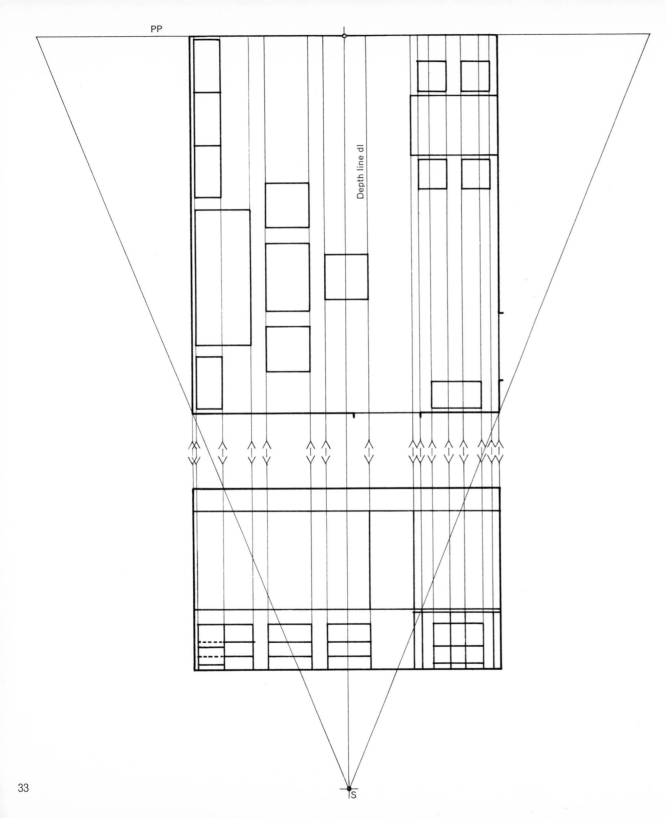

PP

Depth line dl

S

2. The Elevation

Visual rays in the plan are insufficient, because then the heights of the image points are lacking. Each object-point, however, lies on a horizontal line perpendicular to the picture plane, i. e. on a depth line $d\,l$, which can also be represented. The figure formed by the intersections of the depth lines with the picture plane is the elevation, with the scaled widths and heights. This is placed exactly in front of the plan. By means of it we know one point on each depth line. Since straight lines are projected into straight lines, and since straight lines can be drawn only when two points on them are known, we now still need a further point on each depth line. Fortunately we can assert, without introducing any tangible error, that parallel lines intersect at infinity, and we can represent this point common to them all in the perspective.

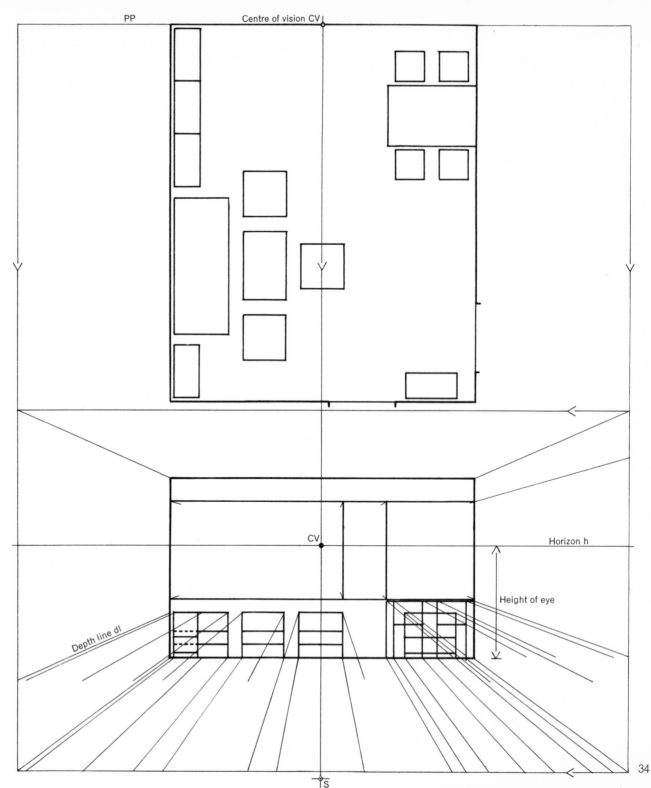

CV

Horizon h

Height of eye

Depth line dl

S

3. The Centre of Vision

The room to be depicted contains lines in only three directions; the depth lines mentioned above and vertical and horizontal lines parallel to the picture plane. Figures in planes parallel to the picture plane will, in the perspective, be changed only in size but not in their angles or length ratios. Lines which are parallel to one another and to the picture plane remain parallel. If we look at points receding further and further away along the depth lines, their images approach closer and closer to the centre of vision, i. e. the point where the picture plane is cut by the principal visual ray (which is parallel to the depth lines). Finally, because of the limits of drawing accuracy, they will coincide with it: the centre of vision, at the centre of the picture and at eye-level on the horizon, is the vanishing point of the depth lines. The perspective images of all the depth lines are drawn outwards from the centre of vision to the appropriate points of the elevation drawing.

34

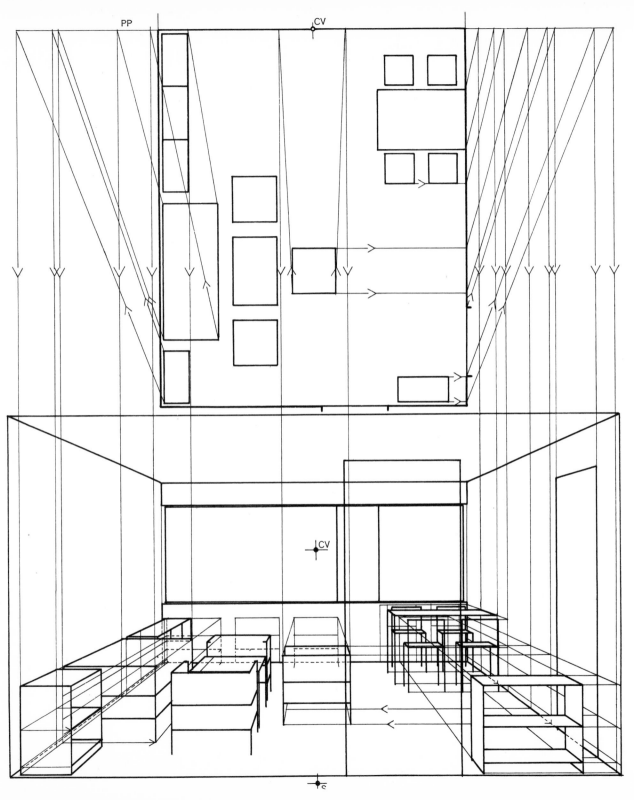

4. The Picture

The image points along PP in the plan (which were obtained by projecting object-points along the visual rays from S on to PP) are transferred downwards parallel to the principal visual ray until the corresponding depth lines are reached. The connecting lines still missing are the images of the object-edges which are parallel to the picture plane; these could now be drawn parallel to the horizontal lines in the elevation. However, the results obtained by this method in the centre of the picture would be inaccurate, because of the small angles between the depth lines and the parallels to the principal visual ray. We therefore first shift object-points in the plan across horizontally to a wall, then project them from the standpoint S on to the picture plane PP, drop verticals from these image points to intersect the appropriate depth lines, and finally shift them back horizontally into the centre of the picture. (This method is easier to carry out than it is to describe; the diagram shows how it is carried out, e.g. for the top corners of the right-hand easy chair.)

Furniture which may be standing obliquely in the room could also be drawn in perspective using the method just described, but at a cost of double the amount of work, and the result would be less accurate than what we could achieve if we bothered to obtain its own vanishing points, as described on pages 42–45. Details such as upholstery and obliquity of chairlegs can be drawn in freehand.

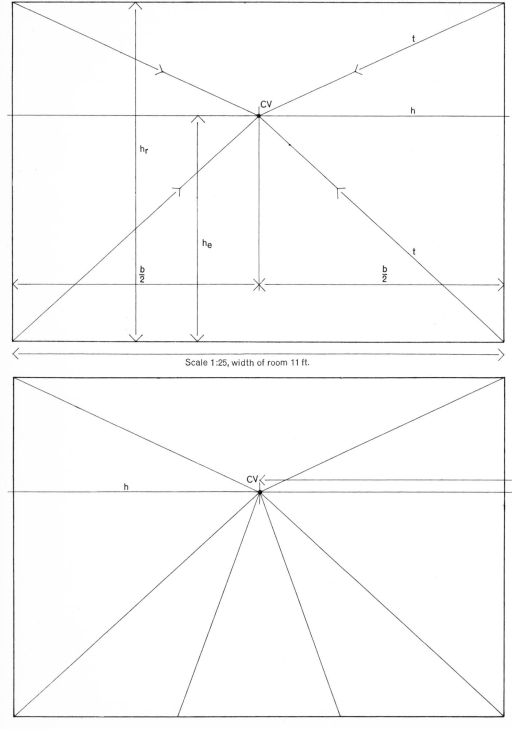

Scale 1:25, width of room 11 ft.

1. Cross-section of a room

A central perspective drawn without using a plan is developed from a cross-section of the room about equal in size to the intended picture size.

Here the scale is taken as 1:25; the room is 3.38 m. (12 ft.) wide and 2.25 m. (7 ft. 6 in.) high. The height of eye h_e is 1.50 m. (5 ft.); h_e should be chosen as a simple numerical ratio of the height of the room h_r, and here we have taken the ratio to be 2:3. The horizon h is drawn at eye-level, 1.50 m. (5 ft.), and the centre of vision CV is placed at the mid-point of the horizon. All depth lines dl are drawn to pass through this point CV; these lines are, of course, really perpendicular to the cross-section of the room.

To place the centre of vision away from the centre of the picture and thus to display one side of the room more prominently is easy but incorrect. To do this properly a diagonal perspective should be drawn.

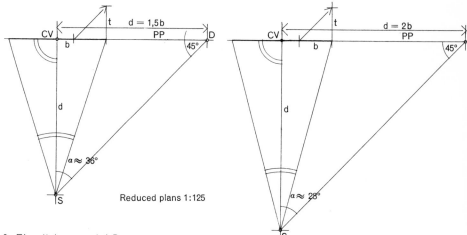

Reduced plans 1:125

2. The distance point D

We now have a picture of the interior of an endless box-like room. Dimensions, including the 'depth' of the room, can be plotted only on some previously chosen scale.

$d = 1\frac{1}{2}$ room width

Actually, we can construct a length along a depth line which is equal to the width of the room in the following way. In the plan such a length would be cut off by a horizontal line inclined at 45° to the breadth. Let us call such a line a 'diagonal'. There is a rule of thumb which states that all lines parallel to the diagonal have a vanishing point situated on the horizon at a distance 1.5 (or between 1 and 2) times the width of the room cross-section to the right or left of the centre of vision.

The two smaller diagrams show how this rule of thumb arises. The angle of vision which the room cross-section subtends at the observer should be about 30°–40°. Therefore the distance d from the eye to the room cross-section in the picture plane should be about 1.5 times the width of this section. Since the diagonal vanishing point D is produced by a horizontal 'diagonal' from the station point to the picture plane, the distance from CV to D will also be equal to d. For this reason the diagonal vanishing point is also called the *distance point*. If the height of the room is very much greater than the width, the distance point D will correspondingly be chosen further away from the centre of vision.

36

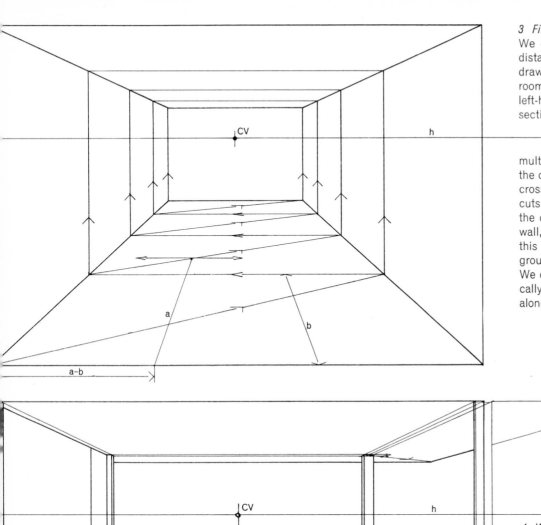

3 Fixing the depth of the room

We draw a line from the front, left-hand corner of the room cross-section to the distance point, and where this cuts the right-hand edge of the room a horizontal is drawn across. The part of the floor thus cut off is in reality a square. If the depth of the room is twice its breadth, another diagonal vanishing line is drawn from the remote left-hand corner of this square, and a second horizontal is drawn at its point of intersection with the right-hand edge, and so on. To obtain a depth which is not an integral multiple of the breadth b, we plot the required depth a along either the floor line or the ceiling line from the right-hand wall towards the left, using the scale of the room cross-section; the line from either of these measuring points to the distance point cuts the corresponding perspective wall edge in the required depth. Alternatively, the construction shown in the figure may be used (plotting $a–b$ from the left-hand wall, joining the measuring point so obtained to CV, and drawing the horizontal where this line cuts the diagonal vanishing line from the remote left-hand corner of the ground square).

We can also construct the depths by plotting a distance point at a distance d vertically above CV and plotting the required depths vertically downward from the ceiling along the trace of the wall.

4. Wall thicknesses, pillars, roof projections

Thicknesses of walls and pillars, roof and window sections, are added to, or inserted in, the room cross-section to scale, and depth-lines are drawn from the corner points of such sections to the centre of vision. If the position of a corner point of the foot or head of a pillar, for example, is known, a horizontal line through this point to the appropriate depth-line gives the pillar width (or the width of a window embrasure similarly); and a diagonal vanishing line through the point gives the depth of the pillar, if the latter is square. The wall thickness of a back wall of the same thickness as the side walls, or the diagonal corner of eaves or roof projections of equal width, are obtained in a similar way. This method is unsuitable for complicated configurations.

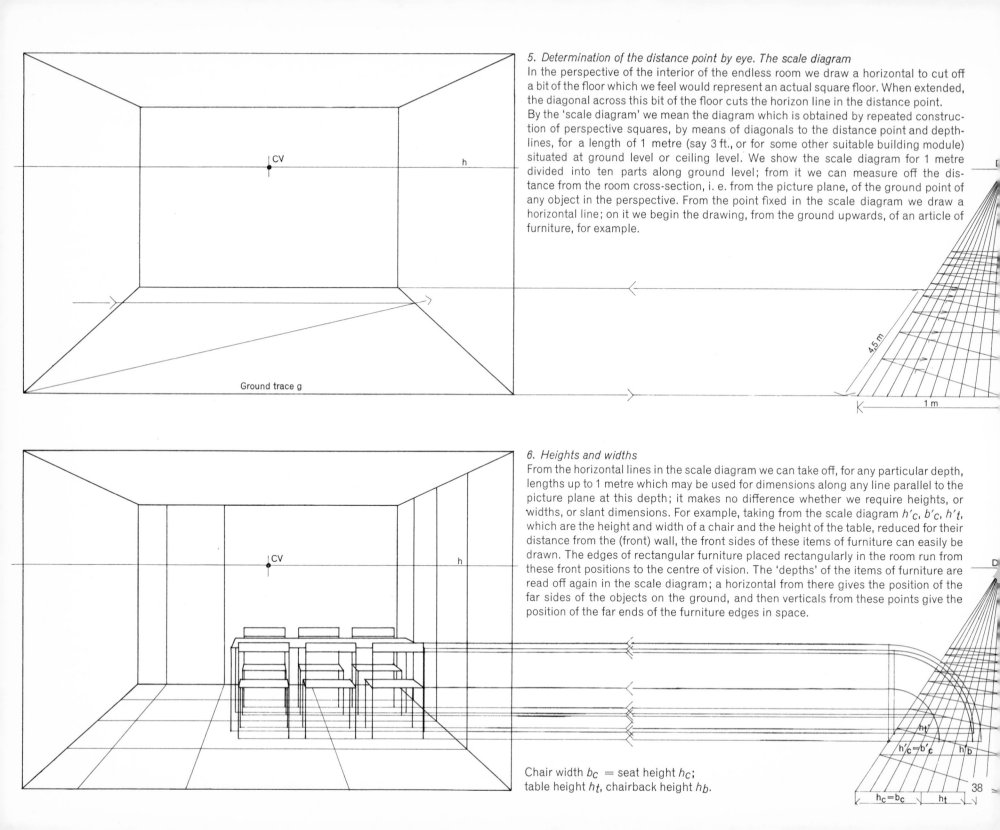

5. Determination of the distance point by eye. The scale diagram

In the perspective of the interior of the endless room we draw a horizontal to cut off a bit of the floor which we feel would represent an actual square floor. When extended, the diagonal across this bit of the floor cuts the horizon line in the distance point.

By the 'scale diagram' we mean the diagram which is obtained by repeated construction of perspective squares, by means of diagonals to the distance point and depthlines, for a length of 1 metre (say 3 ft., or for some other suitable building module) situated at ground level or ceiling level. We show the scale diagram for 1 metre divided into ten parts along ground level; from it we can measure off the distance from the room cross-section, i. e. from the picture plane, of the ground point of any object in the perspective. From the point fixed in the scale diagram we draw a horizontal line; on it we begin the drawing, from the ground upwards, of an article of furniture, for example.

CV

h

Ground trace g

4.5 m

1 m

6. Heights and widths

From the horizontal lines in the scale diagram we can take off, for any particular depth, lengths up to 1 metre which may be used for dimensions along any line parallel to the picture plane at this depth; it makes no difference whether we require heights, or widths, or slant dimensions. For example, taking from the scale diagram h'_c, b'_c, $h't$, which are the height and width of a chair and the height of the table, reduced for their distance from the (front) wall, the front sides of these items of furniture can easily be drawn. The edges of rectangular furniture placed rectangularly in the room run from these front positions to the centre of vision. The 'depths' of the items of furniture are read off again in the scale diagram; a horizontal from there gives the position of the far sides of the objects on the ground, and then verticals from these points give the position of the far ends of the furniture edges in space.

CV

h

D

ht'

$h'_c = b'_c$

h_b

Chair width b_c = seat height h_c;
table height h_t, chairback height h_b.

$h_c = b_c$

h_t

38

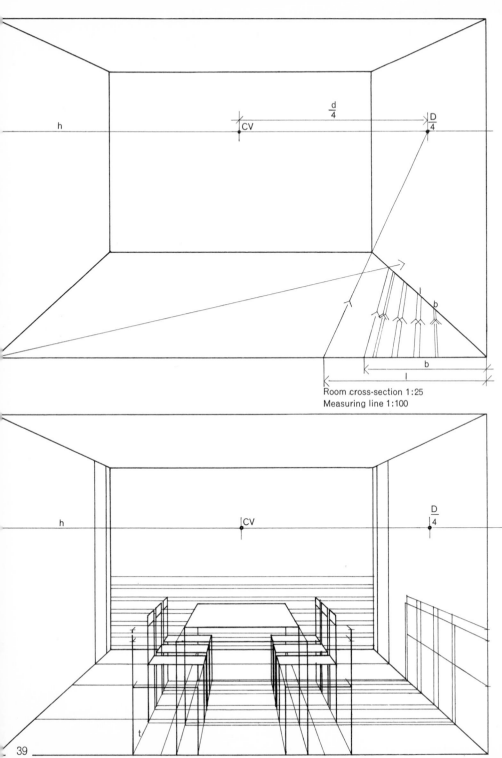

Room cross-section 1:25
Measuring line 1:100

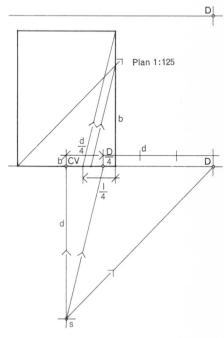

Plan 1:125

7. Partial distance points

The extreme freedom which we have in constructing a central perspective without the use of a plan arises from the fact that in the perspective drawing of the endless interior we can cut off just as much as appears right for the given purpose. We lay off an interval equal to the depth *l* of the room (with subdivisions possibly) on an arbitrary scale from one corner of the room floor section. A line from the free end of this interval to the further corner of the room will then cut the horizon line in a point from which rays to the subdivisions of the interval will cut the whole side edge of the floor in the correct perspective points. If, however, we still want to use the distance point *D* (corresponding to the chosen floor section), we can find it by means of the diagonal in a square bit of the floor, $b \times b$.

Conversely, if we are certain about the distance *d* which we want to use, but then find that the drawing-board is too small to allow us to draw in the distance point—or the depth of the room on the scale of the room cross-section—then we can take an arbitrary fraction of the distance *d*, provided only that the depth of the room plotted along the floor trace is reduced in the same proportion. For example, the partial distance point *D*/4 lies at a distance *d*/4 from *CV*; so the scale of the room cross-section and that of the depth measuring line must be in the ratio 1:4.

8. Construction from the cross-section of the room

Instead of building up the perspective of the furniture in the room by means of the scale diagram, we can start from the cross-section of the room (shown here on the scale 1:25), and plot in on it the furniture to scale, as if a cross-section of it too had been taken. The side edges of the furniture lie along the depth lines *dl* from the corner points to the centre of vision. The depths along the floor are obtained either by means of a partial distance point, as just described, or by horizontals from the scale diagram (see p. 38). Items of furniture standing obliquely are difficult to draw without using a plan. Irregular forms may be enveloped in rectangular forms, and then their perspectives can be drawn in freehand.

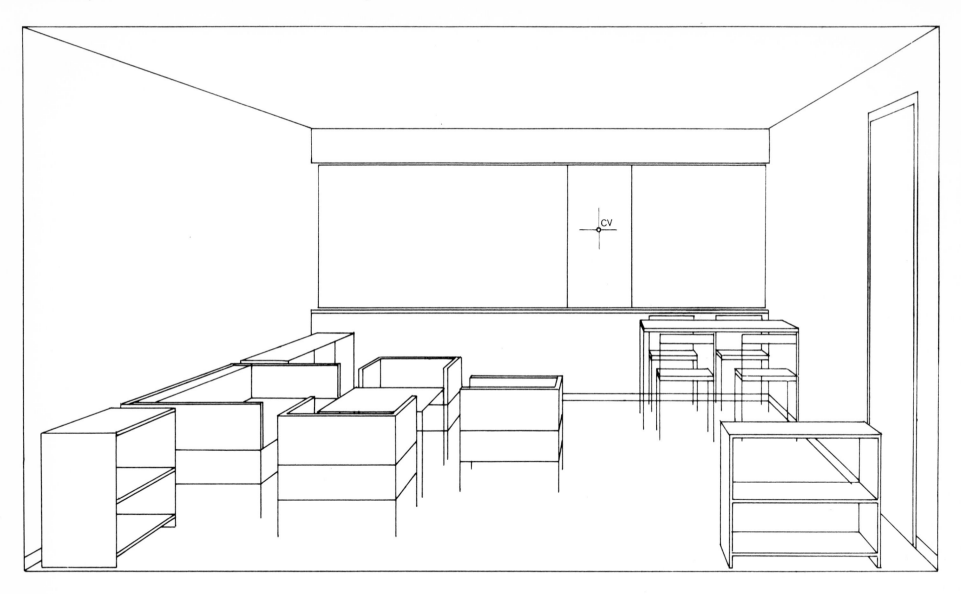

The perspective described on pages 36–39 has been carried out here with the station point shifted sideways. The result corresponds to a wide-angle photograph trimmed unsymmetrically about its centre-line; one side of the picture is distorted in relation to the other.

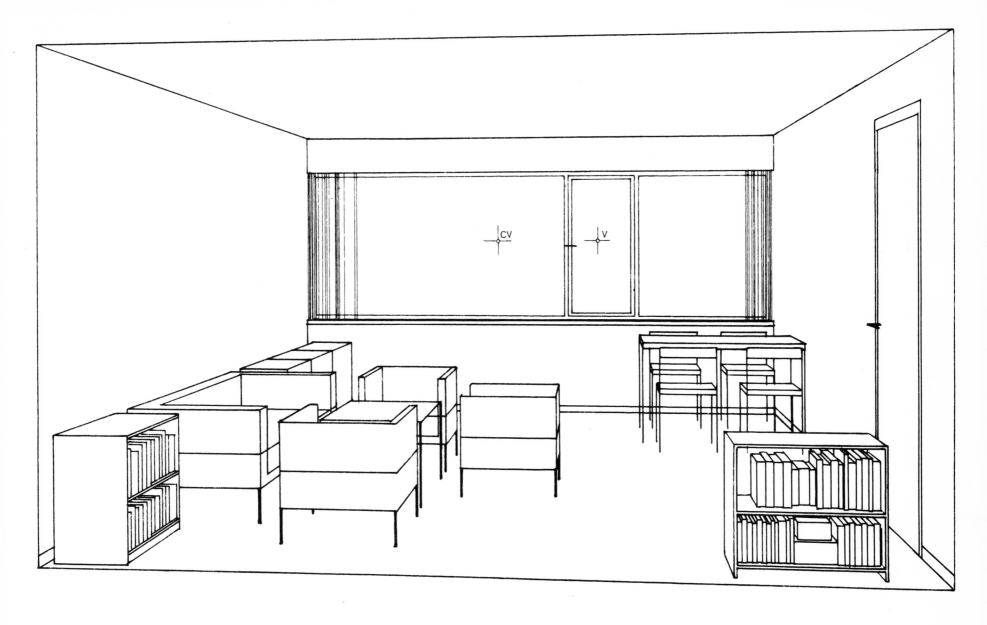

In this very slightly diagonal perspective the room appears less stiff. Diagonal perspective softens the severity of order and symmetry, central perspective penalizes irregularity.

Diagonal Perspective Constructed by Visual Rays

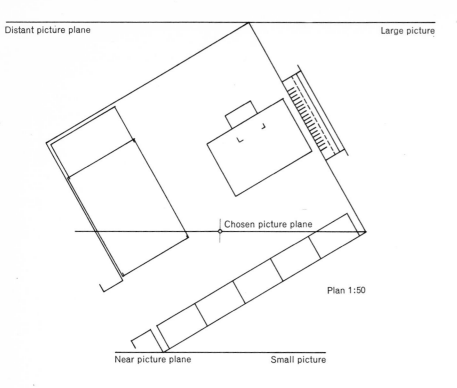

Distant picture plane

Large picture

Chosen picture plane

Plan 1:50

Near picture plane

Small picture

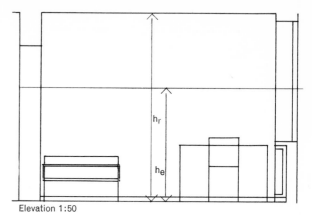

Elevation 1:50

h_r

h_e

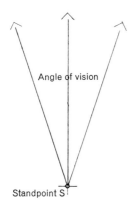

Angle of vision

Standpoint S

To draw a diagonal perspective the plan and elevation of the object must be known. It is advantageous to have these in approximately the same size as the required picture. The plan is rotated into the most suitable position, and a standpoint is chosen in front of it so that everything which is to be shown is included within a visual angle of 30°–45°. A smaller angle gives too distant a view, a greater angle too much distortion (tele- and wide-angle objectives). The principal visual ray is arranged to be parallel to the shortest side of the drawing-board. The picture plane is taken perpendicular to the principal visual ray; an oblique position would introduce unnecessary distortion. The picture is generated as the totality of the points of intersection with the picture plane of the visual rays from points of the object to the station point. The distance between the picture plane and the standpoint determines the picture size, and conversely, in accordance with the properties of similar triangles.

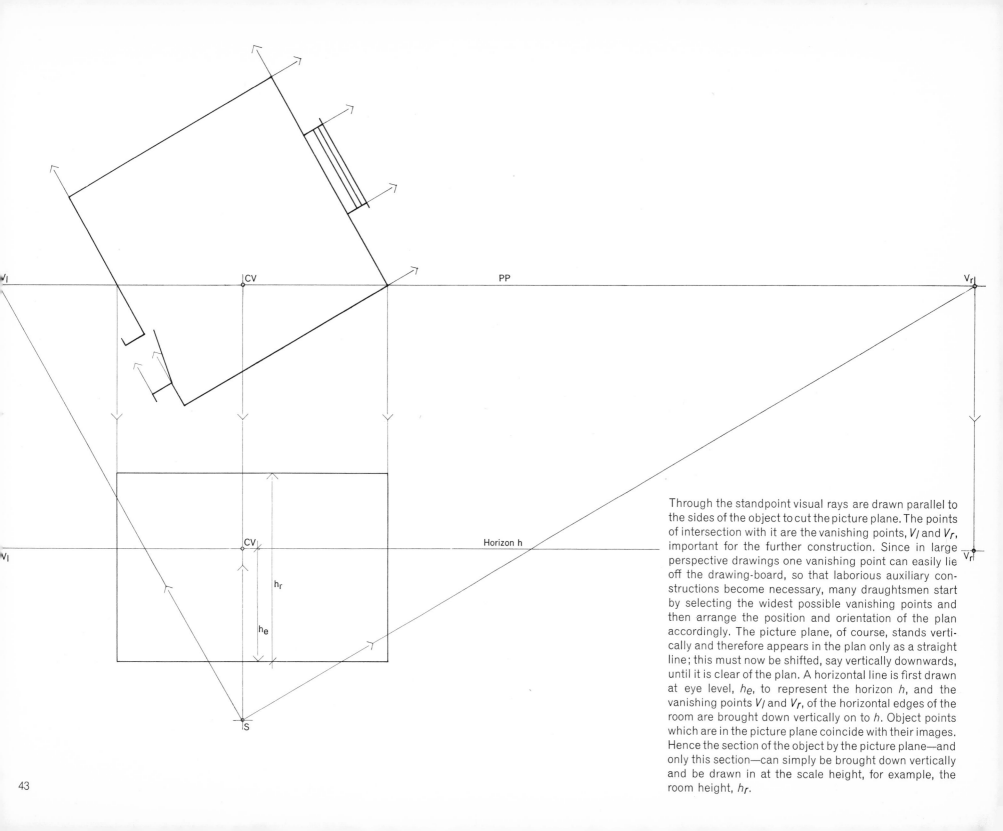

Through the standpoint visual rays are drawn parallel to the sides of the object to cut the picture plane. The points of intersection with it are the vanishing points, V_l and V_r, important for the further construction. Since in large perspective drawings one vanishing point can easily lie off the drawing-board, so that laborious auxiliary constructions become necessary, many draughtsmen start by selecting the widest possible vanishing points and then arrange the position and orientation of the plan accordingly. The picture plane, of course, stands vertically and therefore appears in the plan only as a straight line; this must now be shifted, say vertically downwards, until it is clear of the plan. A horizontal line is first drawn at eye level, h_e, to represent the horizon h, and the vanishing points V_l and V_r, of the horizontal edges of the room are brought down vertically on to h. Object points which are in the picture plane coincide with their images. Hence the section of the object by the picture plane—and only this section—can simply be brought down vertically and be drawn in at the scale height, for example, the room height, h_r.

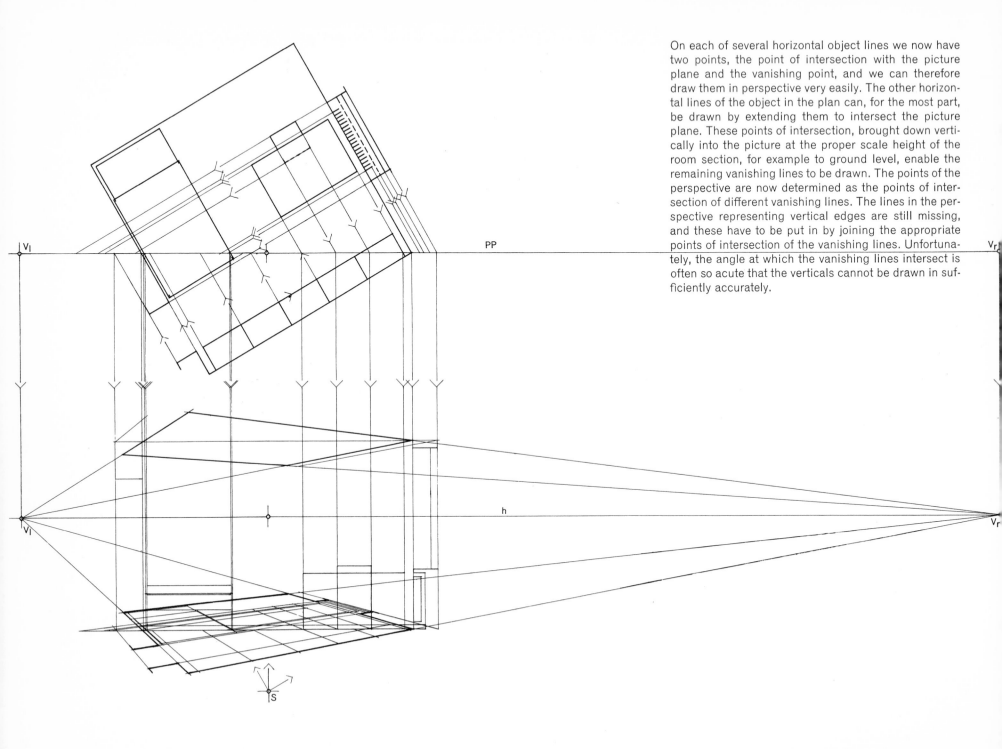

On each of several horizontal object lines we now have two points, the point of intersection with the picture plane and the vanishing point, and we can therefore draw them in perspective very easily. The other horizontal lines of the object in the plan can, for the most part, be drawn by extending them to intersect the picture plane. These points of intersection, brought down vertically into the picture at the proper scale height of the room section, for example to ground level, enable the remaining vanishing lines to be drawn. The points of the perspective are now determined as the points of intersection of different vanishing lines. The lines in the perspective representing vertical edges are still missing, and these have to be put in by joining the appropriate points of intersection of the vanishing lines. Unfortunately, the angle at which the vanishing lines intersect is often so acute that the verticals cannot be drawn in sufficiently accurately.

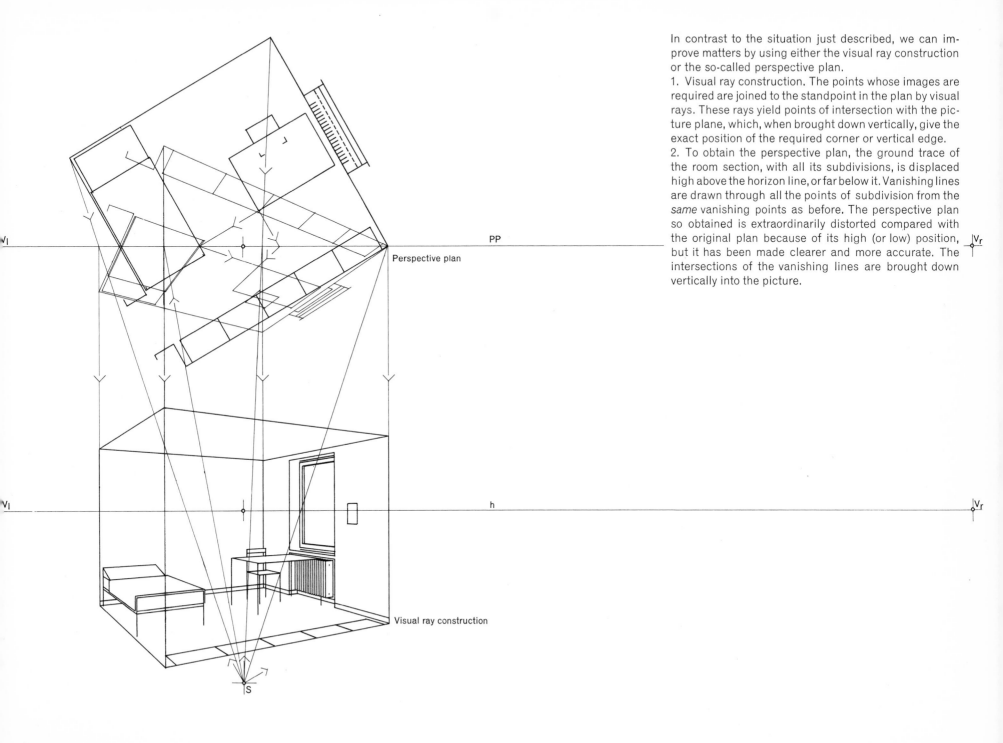

PP

Perspective plan

Visual ray construction

V_l V_r

V_l V_r

h

S

In contrast to the situation just described, we can improve matters by using either the visual ray construction or the so-called perspective plan.

1. Visual ray construction. The points whose images are required are joined to the standpoint in the plan by visual rays. These rays yield points of intersection with the picture plane, which, when brought down vertically, give the exact position of the required corner or vertical edge.

2. To obtain the perspective plan, the ground trace of the room section, with all its subdivisions, is displaced high above the horizon line, or far below it. Vanishing lines are drawn through all the points of subdivision from the *same* vanishing points as before. The perspective plan so obtained is extraordinarily distorted compared with the original plan because of its high (or low) position, but it has been made clearer and more accurate. The intersections of the vanishing lines are brought down vertically into the picture.

Diagonal Perspective Constructed with Measuring Points

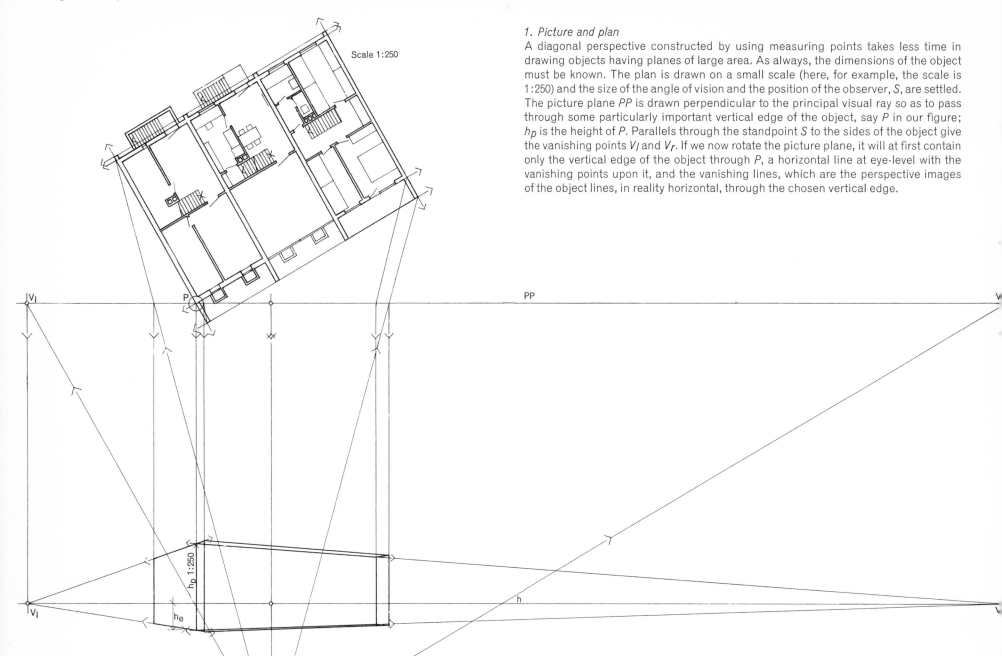

Scale 1:250

1. Picture and plan

A diagonal perspective constructed by using measuring points takes less time in drawing objects having planes of large area. As always, the dimensions of the object must be known. The plan is drawn on a small scale (here, for example, the scale is 1:250) and the size of the angle of vision and the position of the observer, S, are settled. The picture plane PP is drawn perpendicular to the principal visual ray so as to pass through some particularly important vertical edge of the object, say P in our figure; h_p is the height of P. Parallels through the standpoint S to the sides of the object give the vanishing points V_l and V_r. If we now rotate the picture plane, it will at first contain only the vertical edge of the object through P, a horizontal line at eye-level with the vanishing points upon it, and the vanishing lines, which are the perspective images of the object lines, in reality horizontal, through the chosen vertical edge.

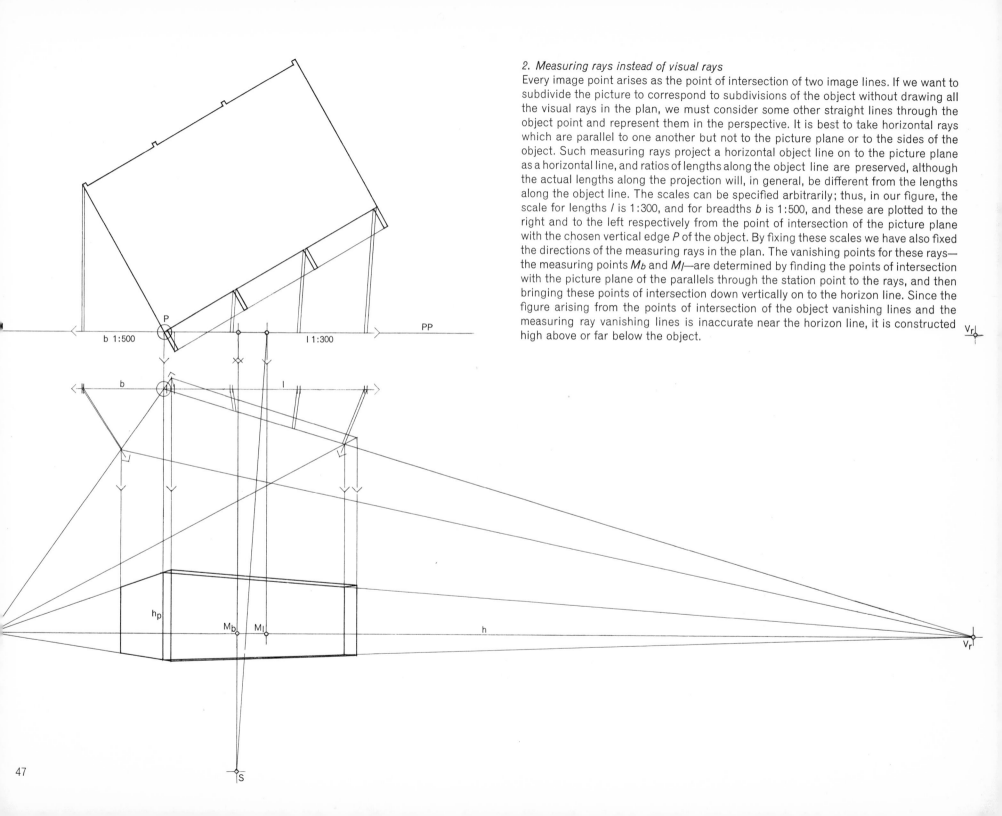

2. Measuring rays instead of visual rays

Every image point arises as the point of intersection of two image lines. If we want to subdivide the picture to correspond to subdivisions of the object without drawing all the visual rays in the plan, we must consider some other straight lines through the object point and represent them in the perspective. It is best to take horizontal rays which are parallel to one another but not to the picture plane or to the sides of the object. Such measuring rays project a horizontal object line on to the picture plane as a horizontal line, and ratios of lengths along the object line are preserved, although the actual lengths along the projection will, in general, be different from the lengths along the object line. The scales can be specified arbitrarily; thus, in our figure, the scale for lengths l is 1:300, and for breadths b is 1:500, and these are plotted to the right and to the left respectively from the point of intersection of the picture plane with the chosen vertical edge P of the object. By fixing these scales we have also fixed the directions of the measuring rays in the plan. The vanishing points for these rays— the measuring points M_b and M_l—are determined by finding the points of intersection with the picture plane of the parallels through the station point to the rays, and then bringing these points of intersection down vertically on to the horizon line. Since the figure arising from the points of intersection of the object vanishing lines and the measuring ray vanishing lines is inaccurate near the horizon line, it is constructed high above or far below the object.

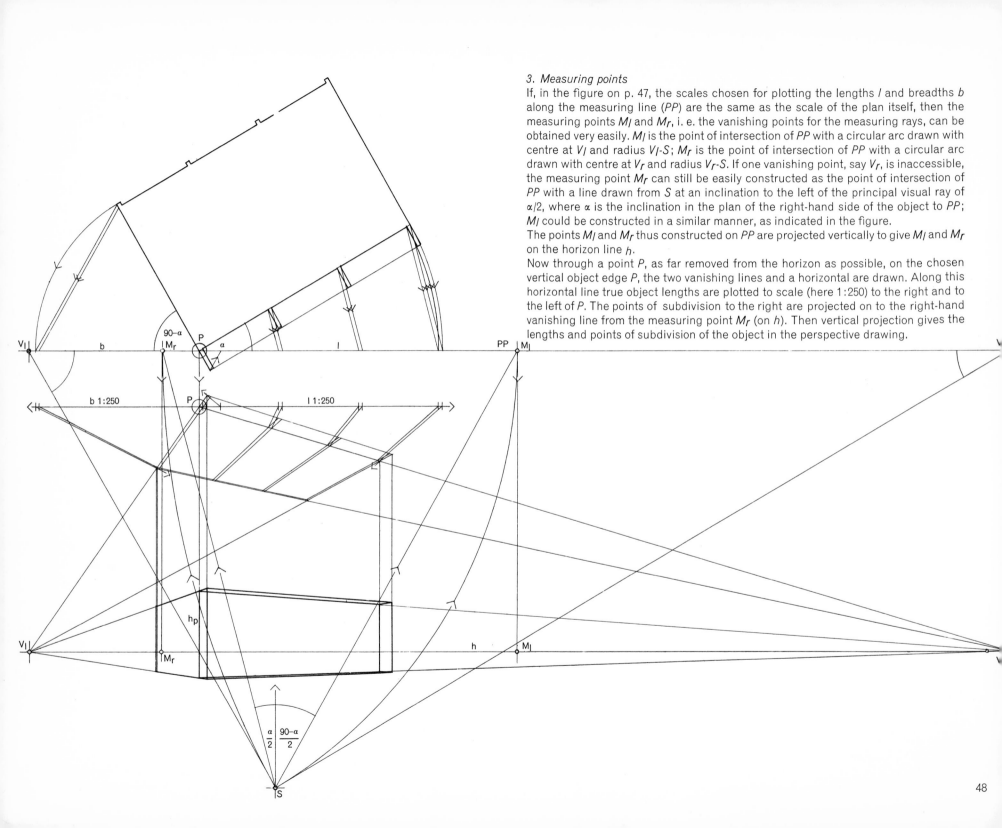

3. Measuring points

If, in the figure on p. 47, the scales chosen for plotting the lengths *l* and breadths *b* along the measuring line (*PP*) are the same as the scale of the plan itself, then the measuring points M_l and M_r, i. e. the vanishing points for the measuring rays, can be obtained very easily. M_l is the point of intersection of *PP* with a circular arc drawn with centre at V_l and radius V_l-*S*; M_r is the point of intersection of *PP* with a circular arc drawn with centre at V_r and radius V_r-*S*. If one vanishing point, say V_r, is inaccessible, the measuring point M_r can still be easily constructed as the point of intersection of *PP* with a line drawn from *S* at an inclination to the left of the principal visual ray of $\alpha/2$, where α is the inclination in the plan of the right-hand side of the object to *PP*; M_l could be constructed in a similar manner, as indicated in the figure.

The points M_l and M_r thus constructed on *PP* are projected vertically to give M_l and M_r on the horizon line *h*.

Now through a point *P*, as far removed from the horizon as possible, on the chosen vertical object edge *P*, the two vanishing lines and a horizontal are drawn. Along this horizontal line true object lengths are plotted to scale (here 1:250) to the right and to the left of *P*. The points of subdivision to the right are projected on to the right-hand vanishing line from the measuring point M_r (on *h*). Then vertical projection gives the lengths and points of subdivision of the object in the perspective drawing.

48

4. Enlargement

A perspective drawing on a scale of 1:250 will generally be too small. In practice, therefore, we construct at most the outline on this small scale and then decide whether the perspective will be satisfactory. If it is, then the picture plane with all the initial points and vanishing points is enlarged to scale. We can extend it as much as

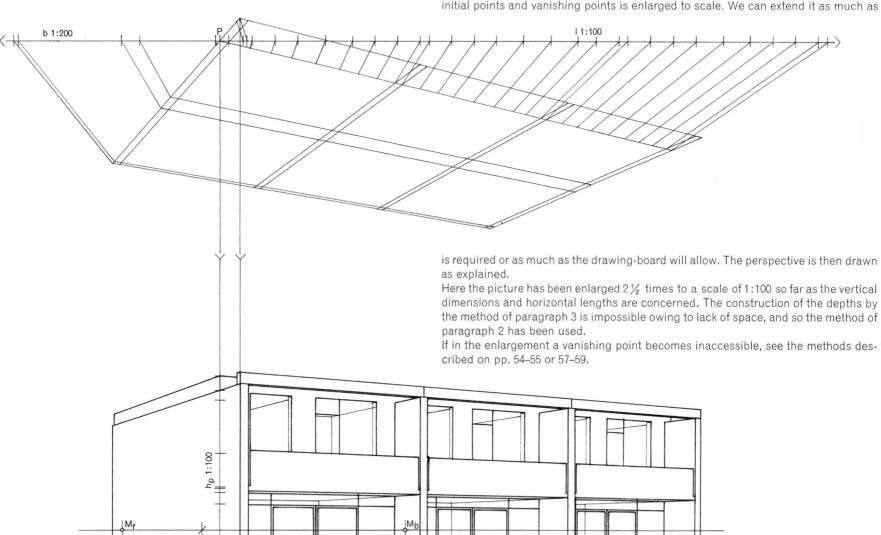

is required or as much as the drawing-board will allow. The perspective is then drawn as explained.

Here the picture has been enlarged 2 ½ times to a scale of 1:100 so far as the vertical dimensions and horizontal lengths are concerned. The construction of the depths by the method of paragraph 3 is impossible owing to lack of space, and so the method of paragraph 2 has been used.

If in the enlargement a vanishing point becomes inaccessible, see the methods described on pp. 54–55 or 57–59.

49

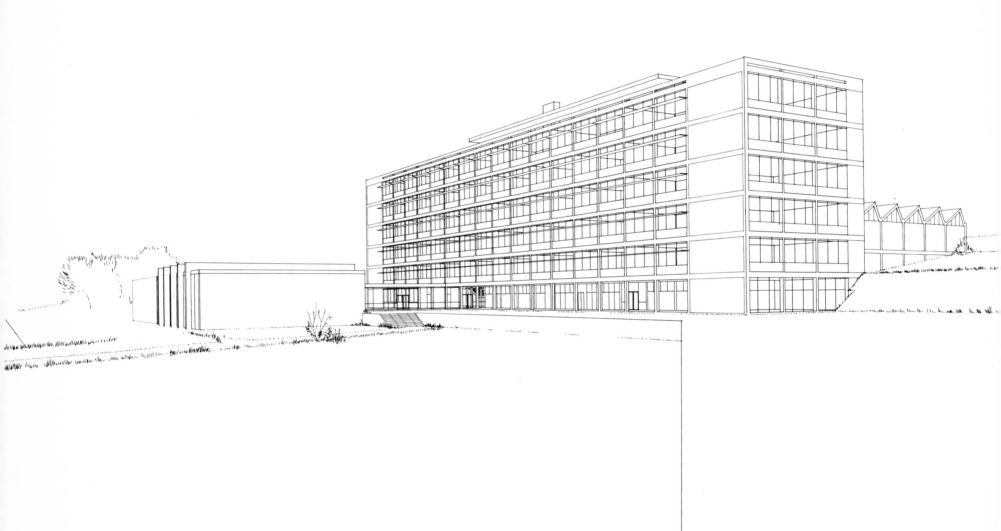

The perspective diagrammatic representation does not look real. We may regard the object of perspective to be to give either a good picture or preferably a good reproduction of reality. The first attitude seeks an immediate, the second a lasting and more general, advantage.

The lines of a perspective drawing have their own individuality. They do not by any means necessarily enhance the similarity to nature of the object portrayed. The shading of the structure cannot simply be continued unaltered from the foreground to the background of the picture; what is near shows its details, the distant only its general form.

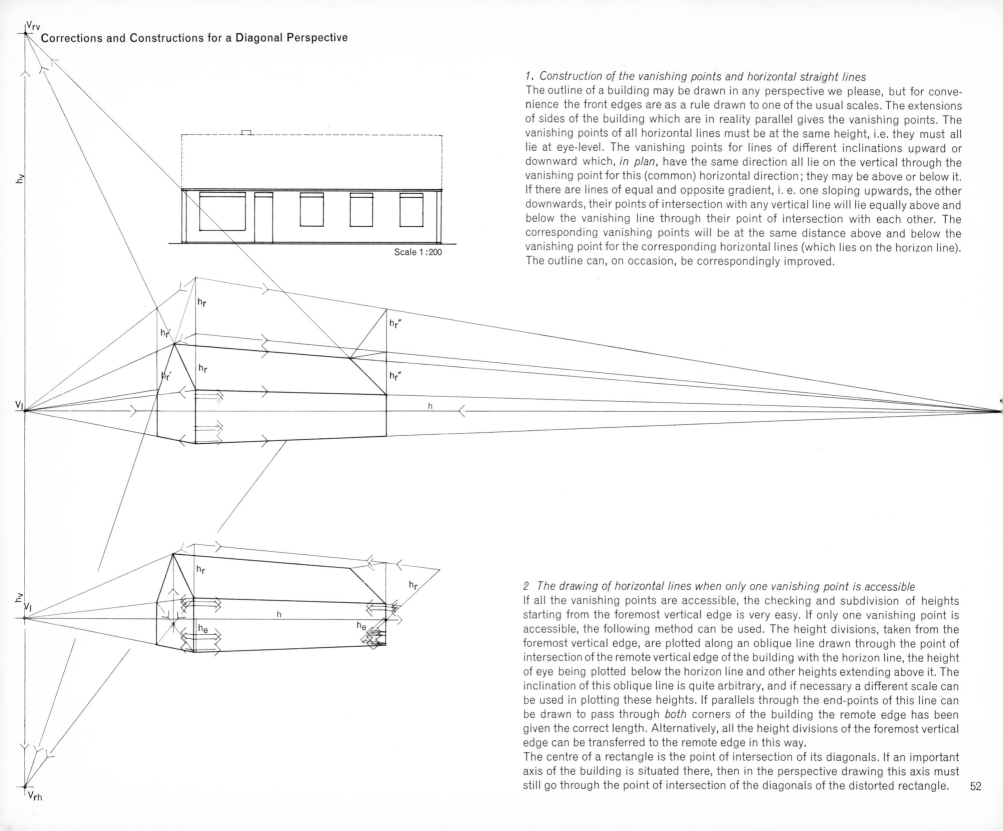

Scale 1:200

1. Construction of the vanishing points and horizontal straight lines
The outline of a building may be drawn in any perspective we please, but for convenience the front edges are as a rule drawn to one of the usual scales. The extensions of sides of the building which are in reality parallel gives the vanishing points. The vanishing points of all horizontal lines must be at the same height, i.e. they must all lie at eye-level. The vanishing points for lines of different inclinations upward or downward which, *in plan*, have the same direction all lie on the vertical through the vanishing point for this (common) horizontal direction; they may be above or below it. If there are lines of equal and opposite gradient, i. e. one sloping upwards, the other downwards, their points of intersection with any vertical line will lie equally above and below the vanishing line through their point of intersection with each other. The corresponding vanishing points will be at the same distance above and below the vanishing point for the corresponding horizontal lines (which lies on the horizon line). The outline can, on occasion, be correspondingly improved.

2 The drawing of horizontal lines when only one vanishing point is accessible
If all the vanishing points are accessible, the checking and subdivision of heights starting from the foremost vertical edge is very easy. If only one vanishing point is accessible, the following method can be used. The height divisions, taken from the foremost vertical edge, are plotted along an oblique line drawn through the point of intersection of the remote vertical edge of the building with the horizon line, the height of eye being plotted below the horizon line and other heights extending above it. The inclination of this oblique line is quite arbitrary, and if necessary a different scale can be used in plotting these heights. If parallels through the end-points of this line can be drawn to pass through *both* corners of the building the remote edge has been given the correct length. Alternatively, all the height divisions of the foremost vertical edge can be transferred to the remote edge in this way.
The centre of a rectangle is the point of intersection of its diagonals. If an important axis of the building is situated there, then in the perspective drawing this axis must still go through the point of intersection of the diagonals of the distorted rectangle.

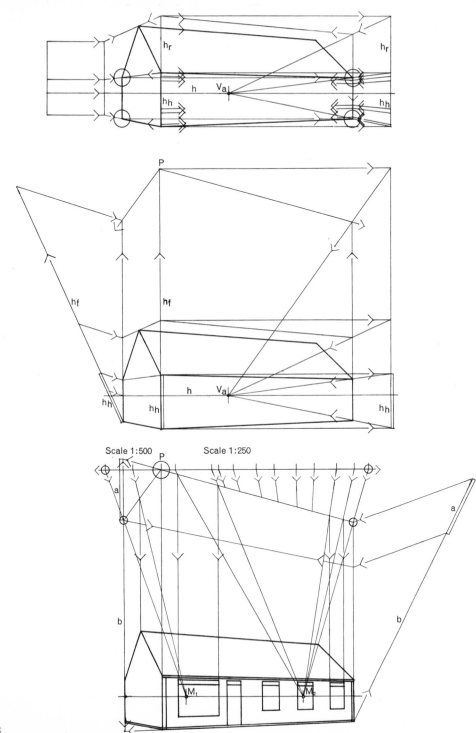

3. Construction of the horizontal lines when no vanishing point is accessible

If all the vanishing points for horizontal lines are inaccessible, we start by drawing two horizontals through the end-points of a vertical edge. In a building these must cut the horizontal cornice and the horizontal floor in two points, one vertically below the other. If this is the case, the foremost edge is shifted sideways, and with two vanishing lines from its ends through the ends of the far edge of the building an auxiliary vanishing point V_a is determined; this also fixes the horizon. The edge of the building may then be subdivided by means of rays through V_a.

An alternative: The outlines can be extended and the foremost edge be drawn in between, on an arbitrary scale; the joins of corresponding points then subdivide the remote edge correctly.

Scale 1 : 200

4. Construction of vertical lines when no vanishing point is accessible

Through a point P on the foremost vertical edge and as far above the horizon as possible, a horizontal line is drawn and two vanishing lines to the extensions of the remoter vertical edges of the building, using if necessary the auxiliary constructions just described to draw these vanishing lines. Along the horizontal line outwards from P the lengths and depths of the object (from the foremost edge) are plotted on any convenient scale. A line is drawn through the last point of division and the end-point of the vanishing line (the ringed points in the diagram) to cut the horizon line in the points M_1 for the depths, M_2 for the lengths. The required vertical lines are drawn through the points of intersection of the rays from the centre M_2 with the corresponding vanishing line; and M_1 is used similarly.

With further vanishing lines, constructed if necessary by the auxiliary construction, a sort of perspective plan can be constructed; its subdivisions are brought down vertically as already described.

Diagonal Perspective drawn by using Paper Strips

1. By this method of construction perspectives can be drawn occupying almost half the drawing-board area, or, if the radial arms (see pages 57–59) are used, occupying almost the entire drawing-board. If a second board is available, the work on the plan can be carried out on the one board and the perspective drawn on the other without extra effort, and this has the advantage of giving a particularly clean drawing. The paper strips used in the construction, if preserved, enable a quick repetition of the drawing to be made without tracing, if for instance the first drawing has been left in pencil but has been spoilt during the water-colouring process. For this method of construction with paper strips the plan and elevation must be prepared in about picture size. The object plan and the standpoint S are located on board 1 so that the angle of vision is about 30°. The orientation of the plan in the angle of vision is determined by the view which it is desired to show in the perspective. The picture plane PP is arranged to form an isosceles triangle in the angle of vision; PP is the base of this triangle and is located to give the desired picture width.

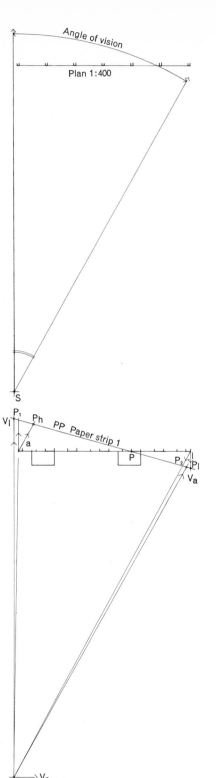

2. Along the trace of the picture plane a straight strip, about $1/2$ in. wide, of strong drawing paper or cardboard is fixed. Along its edge are marked firstly the points of intersection, P, Pl, of the picture plane with the object line (which may in some cases be extended), and also the corresponding vanishing points Vl and Vr. If all the vanishing points are accessible, this suffices for the time being. With large perspectives, however, Vr is usually inaccessible. The extreme object points must then, in addition, be projected on to the picture plane as the points P_1 and P_2. Object lines which in the plan point almost to the standpoint S must be replaced by auxiliary lines, since they would not yield usable results in the picture. These auxiliary lines are directed so that their vanishing point lies on the opposite edge of the picture (a, Va).

3. The object, say the plan of the ground floor, is mapped on to the picture plane, i. e. on to the paper strip, by visual rays, straight lines drawn from the standpoint S. To avoid errors these points of intersection may be distinguished by reference letters or numbers.

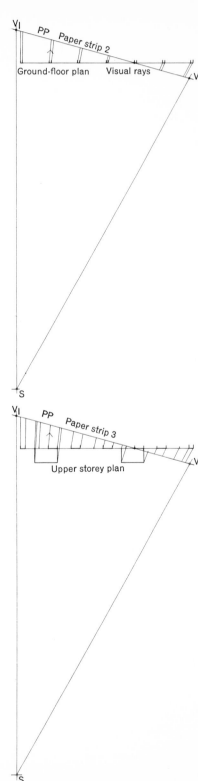

4. If necessary, new paper strips can be attached for each new storey. Each of these paper strips must generally be marked with one or two of the fixed points, for example, the vanishing points Vl and Va for object lines and auxiliary lines, so that they always come into the picture in the right position. The plans of the various storeys must also fit exactly one over the other and be fixed always in the same position.

54

5. A drawing sheet corresponding to the width of the picture is attached to drawing-board 2, and on it the position of the horizon h is settled. On to this line the points from paper strip 1 are plotted and verticals drawn through these. Heights along verticals common to the picture plane and the object are taken from an elevation or section which has been drawn to the same scale and which may, for this purpose, be attached to the board so that the line h is at the desired eye-level, h_e.

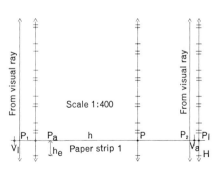

Scale 1:400

Paper strip 1

6. Through the points vertically above P_a lines are drawn from V_a, and through the points vertically above P_l lines are drawn from V_l. The points of intersection of the vanishing lines with the verticals through the visual-ray points P_1 and P_2 from paper strip 1 are accordingly joined to one another or to the points of intersection of object and picture plane which appear on the vertical above P. Hence we obtain the images f of all horizontals such as floor levels, parapet railings, and so on.

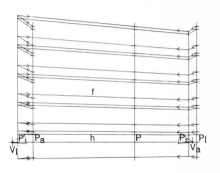

7. Paper strip 2 is placed horizontally below the horizon so that the vanishing points fit. The verticals through its points of subdivision give the positions for the uprights on the ground floor. Similarly paper strip 3 is attached along the horizon so that the vanishing points fit; the verticals through its points of subdivision give the positions of the verticals for window frames and edges of balconies on the upper floor.

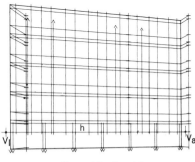

Paper strips 2 and 3

8. The horizontal side edges of the balconies are vanishing lines drawn, from the left-hand vanishing point V_l, from the points of intersection of the further balcony verticals with the parapet horizontals and lintel lines up to the nearer balcony verticals. The nearer balcony horizontals are obtained by joining the side corner-points.

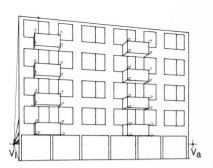

The 'Reile' T-square

A practical device for drawing perspectives is the 'Reile' T-square (named after its inventor), which, if of the dimensions shown in the diagram, is suitable for drawing perspectives up to about 35×35 cm. (12 × 12 in.).

One can easily make the device oneself. It is designed to reduce to a single, foolproof operation the process of lining up on the object and bringing the point down vertically, by means of a rotatable and sliding attachment of a lath to a pin which is placed in the chosen standpoint, with a T-square attached to the lath by an articu-

lated joint. Since, however, the drawing board can then be used only along its length, more often than not one of the vanishing points will be inaccessible; so that more work is required for heights, which have to be turned round parallel to the picture plane and increased.

The most important of its uses.

T-square 1 extends across the picture plane. The centre of the pivot is situated at the point where lines drawn along the edge of the T-square and the lath would inter-

sect. The locus of this point as the T-square is shifted along the edge of the drawing-board determines the trace PP of the picture plane. The plan (here on a scale of 1:250) is attached in front of the picture plane. The principal ray z is drawn and on it the standpoint S is decided on; a pin is driven in at this point. The position of the horizon in the picture area is settled. The height, h_o, of a point P above the horizon is read off from the elevation (scale 1:250) and is laid off along T-square 2 from the principal ray along the parallel to the picture plane through P in the plan. If the lath lies at the free end of this interval, then the distance of T-square 1 from the principal ray gives the modified height, h'_o, of P in the perspective. T-square 1 is shifted so that the edge of the lath is aligned on P in the plan. The T-square then shows the position of P to the side in the perspective, and the perspective height of P can be plotted along it from the horizon.

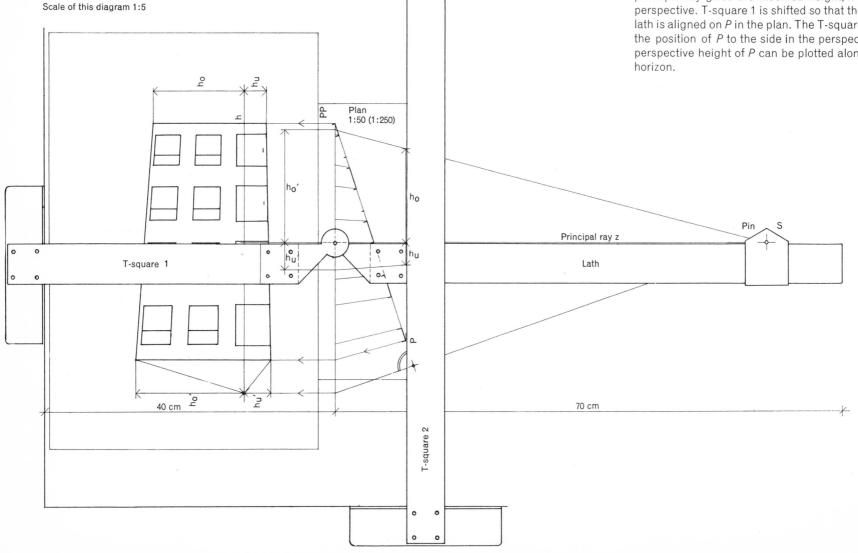

Scale of this diagram 1:5

Plan 1:50 (1:250)

T-square 1

T-square 2

Principal ray z

Lath

Pin   S

40 cm

70 cm

The Arc Protractor

To draw a circular arc of span s and height h we can plot the end-points and vertex and then determine the centre C of the circle by drawing, as on p. 12. The radius r of the circle may be calculated from

$$r^2 - (r-h)^2 = \left(\frac{s}{2}\right)^2 \text{ as } r = \left[\left(\frac{s}{2}\right)^2 + h^2\right]/2h$$

If the centre C is inaccessible, we can insert pins at the end-points of the arc, and make an 'arc protractor'. Two T-squares, each somewhat longer than the arc length, are screwed together through their suspension-holes so that they both touch the vertex of the arc and each blade touches one of the pins. If the T-squares are now moved so that each is always in contact with one of the pins, a pencil placed in the angle formed by the T-squares will trace out the required circular arc. The arc protractor can, of course, be made from laths or strips of cardboard.

Radial Arms

If a third arm is fitted to the arc protractor so that one of its edges, the drawing edge, bisects the reflex angle, then it might be supposed that, when the outer arms 1 and 2 are placed in contact with the points P_1 and P_2, the third arm would always point in the direction of the centre C of the circle whose arc is to be drawn through P_1 and P_2. This is not so. The third arm is always directed towards the point S of the circle which is opposite to the vertex of the arc. But we have thus discovered a device for drawing lines through the inaccessible point of inter-section of two given lines. The radial arms device saves much arduous work in drawing large perspectives or perspectives in which the object is almost parallel to the picture plane. Theoretically, by using this device, we could avoid the need for the standpoint or any of the vanishing points.

A similar device, available from some drawing-instrument suppliers, is the 'A. H. Centrolinead'.

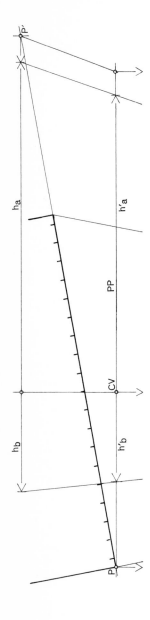

Required: Two strong pins, three laths of smooth pinewood, planed straight and true, about 1.00–1.50 m. (3–4$\frac{1}{2}$ ft.) long, 6–8 cm. (2$\frac{1}{2}$–3 in.) wide, and 4 mm. ($\frac{3}{16}$ in.) thick; also the plan of the object in about the same size as the required picture.

Example: 4-storeyed dwelling house, 19 m. (62 ft.) wide with 18 elements each of 1 m. (3 ft. 3 in.) and 2 elements of 0.50 m. (20 in.), socle 1.20 m. (4 ft.), storey height 2.80 m. (9 ft.), window breasts 0.80 m. (32 in.), floor thickness 0.30 m. (12 in.), window height 1.70 m. (5 ft. 7 in.).

The starting point for the perspective, the plan with the picture plane PP and the standpoint S are laid off, here on a scale of 1:200, and the line of the façade, which deviates only slightly from the picture plane, is defined by the two points P and P' as far away from one another as possible. The point P lies in the picture plane. A line is drawn through P horizontally to the right, and on this line an arbitrary height is plotted, made up of h_b below the horizon and h_a above the horizon, which is shown in the diagram as a vertical line; h_a and h_b should be as large as possible or as large as necessary for the perspective.

Next a horizontal line is drawn through the image of the point P', i. e. through the point of intersection of the line SP' with the picture plane PP. To obtain the height of the image of P', a line is drawn through P' parallel to the picture plane. This line is divided into two parts by the principal visual ray, the line from the standpoint S to the centre of vision CV. We plot h_a above the point of intersection, h_b below it. Then the visual rays from S to the free ends of these h_a and h_b intervals cut off on the picture plane the image heights h'_a and h'_b for P' above and below the horizon. We thus obtain the points A' and B'. The straight lines f joining the height h_a and the image height h'_a, and the height h_b and image height h'_b, are vanishing lines through the inaccessible vanishing point. We take A' as the first contact point when we use the radial arms. At A' we draw a line parallel to the lower vanishing line and bisect the angle so formed; then we draw a line through the vertex perpendicular to this bisector, i.e. we construct the external bisector of the angle. The point of intersection of this external bisector with the lower vanishing line is the second contact point, B, which we need when using the radial arms.

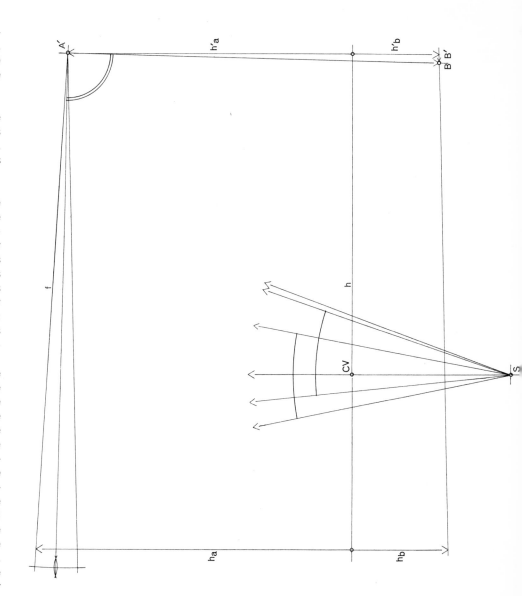

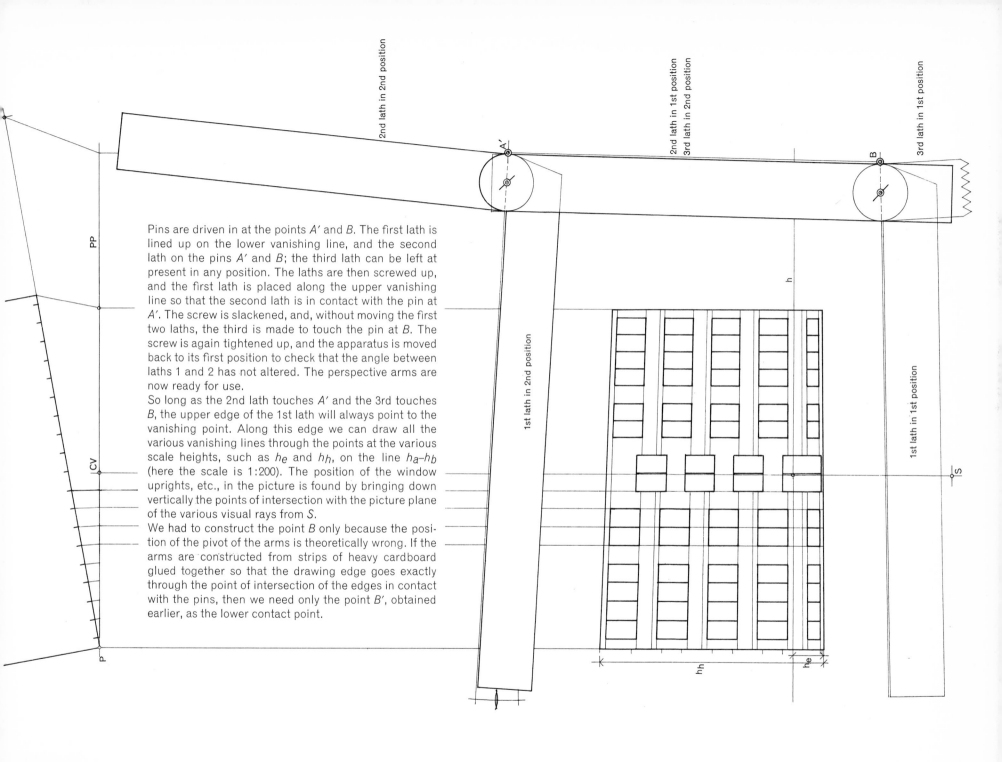

2nd lath in 2nd position

A'

2nd lath in 1st position
3rd lath in 2nd position

B

3rd lath in 1st position

PP

h

1st lath in 2nd position

CV

S

P

Pins are driven in at the points A′ and B. The first lath is lined up on the lower vanishing line, and the second lath on the pins A′ and B; the third lath can be left at present in any position. The laths are then screwed up, and the first lath is placed along the upper vanishing line so that the second lath is in contact with the pin at A′. The screw is slackened, and, without moving the first two laths, the third is made to touch the pin at B. The screw is again tightened up, and the apparatus is moved back to its first position to check that the angle between laths 1 and 2 has not altered. The perspective arms are now ready for use.

So long as the 2nd lath touches A′ and the 3rd touches B, the upper edge of the 1st lath will always point to the vanishing point. Along this edge we can draw all the various vanishing lines through the points at the various scale heights, such as h_e and h_h, on the line h_a–h_b (here the scale is 1:200). The position of the window uprights, etc., in the picture is found by bringing down vertically the points of intersection with the picture plane of the various visual rays from S.

We had to construct the point B only because the position of the pivot of the arms is theoretically wrong. If the arms are constructed from strips of heavy cardboard glued together so that the drawing edge goes exactly through the point of intersection of the edges in contact with the pins, then we need only the point B′, obtained earlier, as the lower contact point.

1st lath in 1st position

h_h

h_e

59

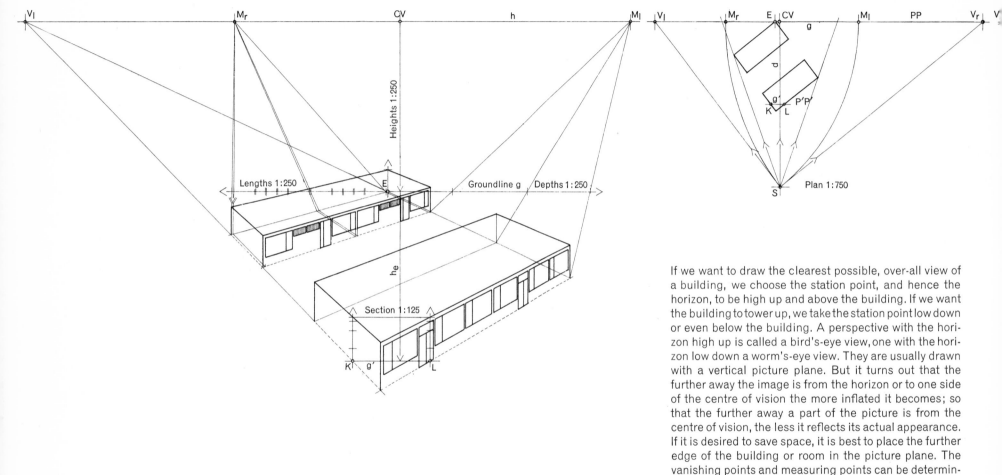

Labels in the figure:

V_l · M_r · CV · h · M_l · | V_l | M_r · E · CV · M_l · PP · V_r · V

Heights 1:250

Lengths 1:250 · E · Groundline g · Depths 1:250

h_e

Section 1:125

K · g' · L

Plan 1:750 · S

If we want to draw the clearest possible, over-all view of a building, we choose the station point, and hence the horizon, to be high up and above the building. If we want the building to tower up, we take the station point low down or even below the building. A perspective with the horizon high up is called a bird's-eye view, one with the horizon low down a worm's-eye view. They are usually drawn with a vertical picture plane. But it turns out that the further away the image is from the horizon or to one side of the centre of vision the more inflated it becomes; so that the further away a part of the picture is from the centre of vision, the less it reflects its actual appearance. If it is desired to save space, it is best to place the further edge of the building or room in the picture plane. The vanishing points and measuring points can be determined using a plan drawn on the scale 1:750, and their distances from CV are then multiplied by 3 to give their positions in the picture drawn to scale 1:250. Object-lengths lying in the plane P'P' parallel to the picture plane and halfway between the standpoint and the picture plane will appear twice as great as equal object-lengths lying in the picture plane. The images of the ground-points K and L on P'P' will lie on the ground-line g' situated at a distance $2 \times h_e$ below the horizon; and from the image points of K and L we can lay off height-lines, width-lines and depth-lines on the scale 1:125. The measuring points and depth points remain the same as before.

60

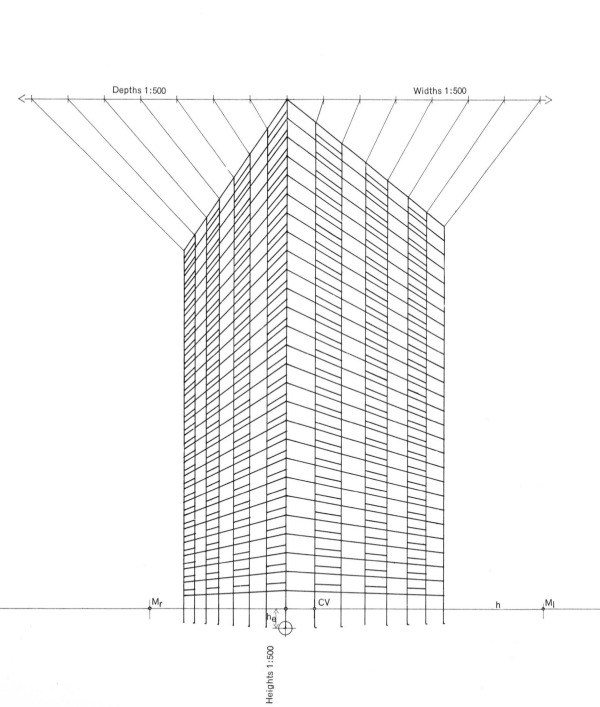

Depths 1:500

Widths 1:500

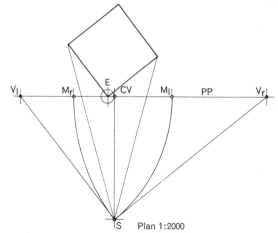

Plan 1:2000

Heights 1:500

From a small plan—here drawn on the scale 1:2000—the points of the intersection of the picture plane with the object, and the vanishing points and measuring points are determined, and also the necessary magnification, here fourfold. The mutual distances of these points are worked out accordingly and plotted on an arbitrary horizontal line. At the point on this horizontal corresponding to the point E, the height of eye, h_e, is plotted vertically downwards, on the scale $1 : \dfrac{2000}{4} = 1 : 500$, and from the point so obtained the height of the building is plotted upwards. The vanishing lines are drawn from the upper corner of the building, and these are subdivided per-

spectively by rays from the measuring points M_l and M_r to the appropriate points of subdivision for widths and depths plotted along the horizontal line through the top corner of the building. Verticals through the points of subdivision on the vanishing lines, and further vanishing lines from the front edge of the building, enable its division into blocks to be completed.

Frontal Bird's-eye View, Constructed using Measuring Points

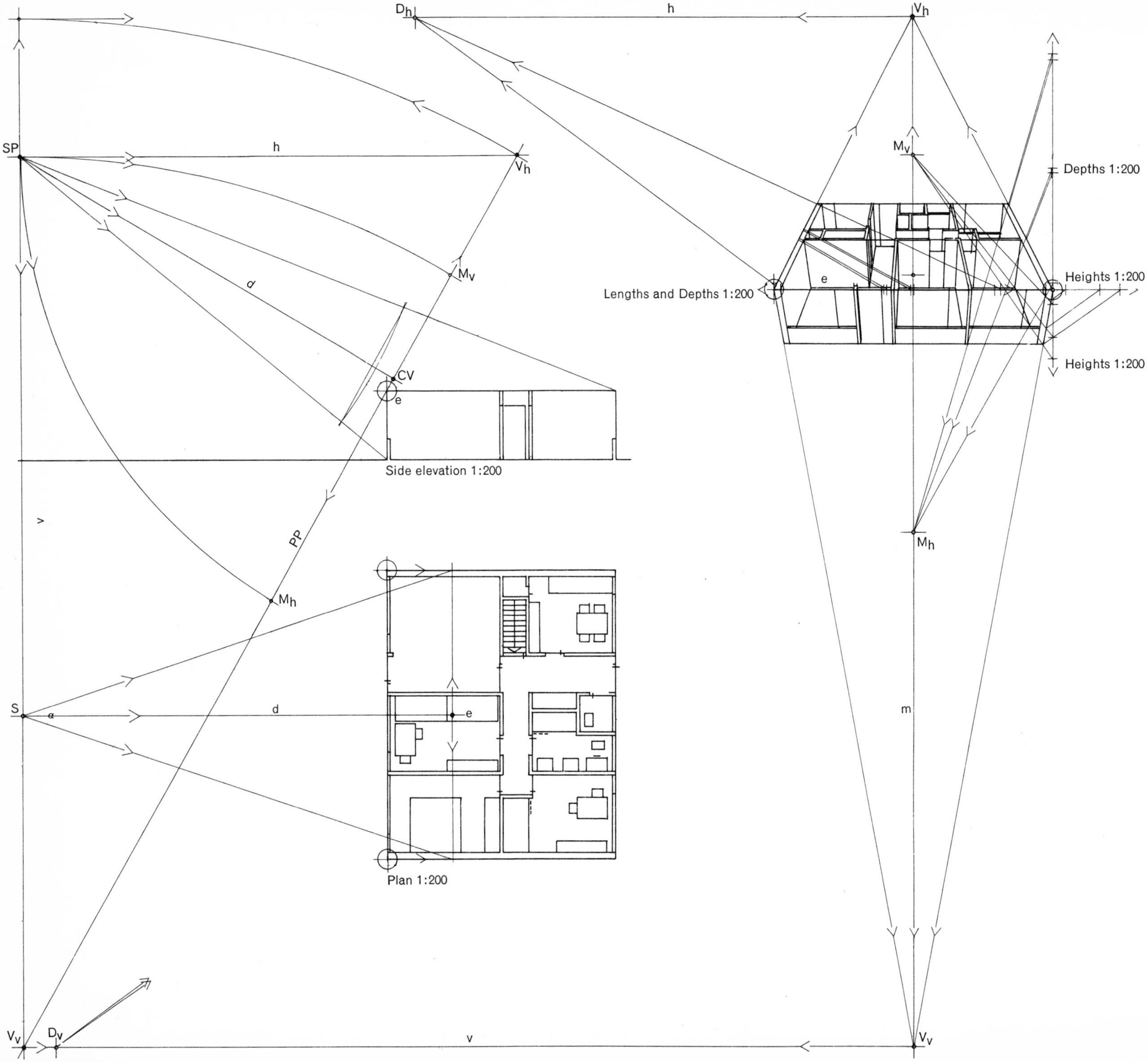

Dh
h
Vh
SP
h
Vh
Mv
d
CV
e
Side elevation 1:200
v
PP
Mh
S
α
d
e
Plan 1:200
Vv
Dv
v
Vv
Mv
Depths 1:200
Heights 1:200
Lengths and Depths 1:200
e
Heights 1:200
Mh
m

Frontal Worm's-eye View, Constructed using Visual Rays

Given: Side elevation, and dimensions of front elevation; scale here is 1:500.

This, too, is a construction which is rarely carried out. The angle of vision, of about 30°, is intersected by the picture plane PP so that an isosceles triangle is formed. The side elevation of the building is arranged, if possible with a dimensioned edge in the picture plane, so that it lies within the angle of vision and so that the station point is at a possible and probable position in the building site. Lines drawn through the station point parallel to the edges of the building fix the positions of the vanishing points V_h and V_v on the picture plane PP. These are transferred across horizontally on to the axis m of the picture, which is parallel to PP. The dimensioned object-edge lying on PP is now put into the picture as a line perpendicular to m and dimensions are marked along it to scale. Vanishing lines from V_v to this dimensioned edge determine the perspective verticals. The horizontals are drawn through the points of intersection with PP of the visual rays drawn from the station point to the object (the side elevation), and so the picture is obtained. The horizon of the picture runs horizontally through V_h. For large pictures the picture axis, m' must be taken parallel to the longer edge of the drawing-board.

Opposite page:
The rarely used frontal bird's-eye view is constructed like an edgewise diagonal perspective. We start from the side elevation. A station point SP is selected above and to one side of the cross-section of the building so that the angle of vision embracing the object does not exceed 30°. The cone of vision is drawn and a third side constructed to form an isosceles triangle. The picture plane is drawn parallel to this third side through the edge e of the object. The vanishing points V_v (for verticals) and V_h (for horizontals) are found by drawing lines through the station point parallel to the sides of the object and locating their intersections with the picture plane. The corresponding measuring points M_v and M_h are then determined as usual, e. g. by making V_v to M_v equal to the distance V_v to SP.

The distances determined from the side elevation along the picture plane are plotted along the perpendicular to the picture axis, m. The perspective picture is constructed from the horizontal edge e of the object by means of the vanishing lines, measuring points and the perpendicular measuring lines. If the intersections are too vague because the angles between lines are too acute, the measurements along the horizontal edge e can also be plotted, and the heights, by means of rays from the distance point D_v situated at a transverse distance v from V_v, and the depths, by rays from the distance point D_h at a transverse distance h from V_h, are determined using the appropriate vanishing lines. It can be checked from the plan that the angle of vision α determined by the distance d (between SP and CV) and by the length l is not too great in the transverse direction.

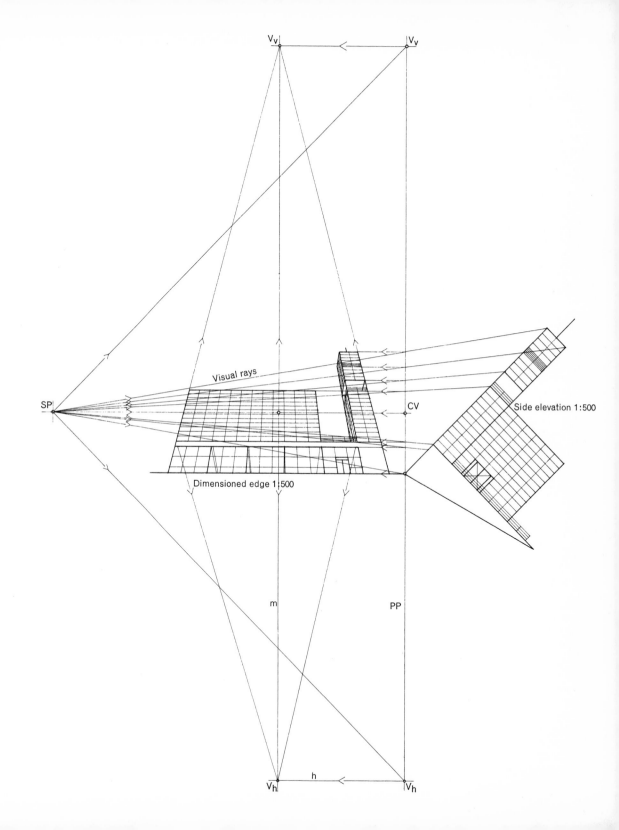

Side elevation 1:500

Visual rays

Dimensioned edge 1:500

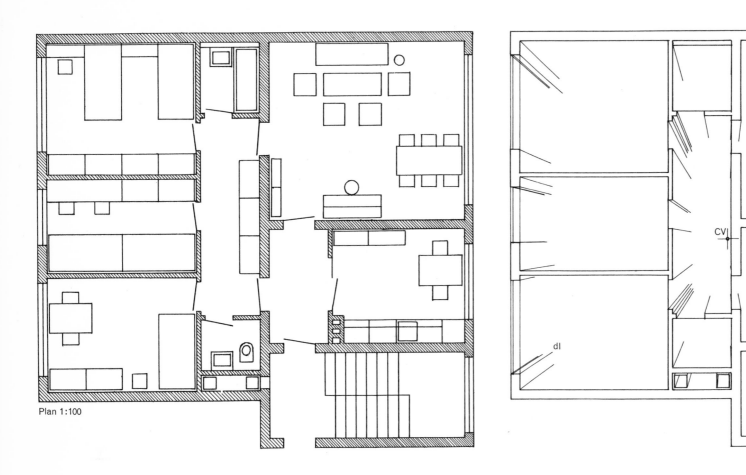

Plan 1:100

Pictures whose principal visual ray is vertical and whose picture plane is therefore horizontal start from the plan (given in this example on the scale 1:100), and are nothing more or less than central perspectives: either ground perspectives from above, or ceiling perspectives from below. In them all horizontal outlines—rectangles, circles, stars, sinuous curves—appear in their original proportions. Only the sizes are changed, and those of objects at the same height are changed in the same ratio. The centre of vision CV is placed at the centre, or at the 'centre of gravity', of the plan. All the depth-lines run towards it; if the perspective is downwards, anything below the picture plane will be situated on the inward part of a depth-line, and anything above the picture plane on the depth-line extended outwards.

Opposite page:
To determine heights, an elevation must be drawn below the plan, and in it the positions of the picture plane PP and of the station point SP above it are plotted, these positions being fixed by the position of the centre of vision CV which has already been drawn and by the desired angle of vision α. But since we have little actual experience of ground perspectives, we can let α be as much as 45° without risk of producing a sense of distortion.
We find the points of intersection with PP of the visual rays from CV to the various points in the elevation; the verticals through these points of intersection to the appropriate depth-lines dl determine the lengths of the various vertical edges in the perspective.
However, this construction is impossible for objects

which lie directly on the line SP to CV, and will be inaccurate for objects situated near this line. For such objects we therefore use a method similar to that already explained on p. 35. The object-point is shifted horizontally in both the plan and elevation on to an object-wall (or on to some auxiliary wall) which appears vertically in both plan and elevation. The point so obtained in the plan is joined to CV by a depth-line. The point obtained in the elevation is joined to SP by a visual ray; where this visual ray cuts the picture plane a vertical is erected. The point of intersection of this vertical with the depth-line already drawn is then shifted back horizontally on to the depth-line through its original position. Parallels to the lines in the plan drawn through the points of intersection already found on the depth-lines complete the picture.

64

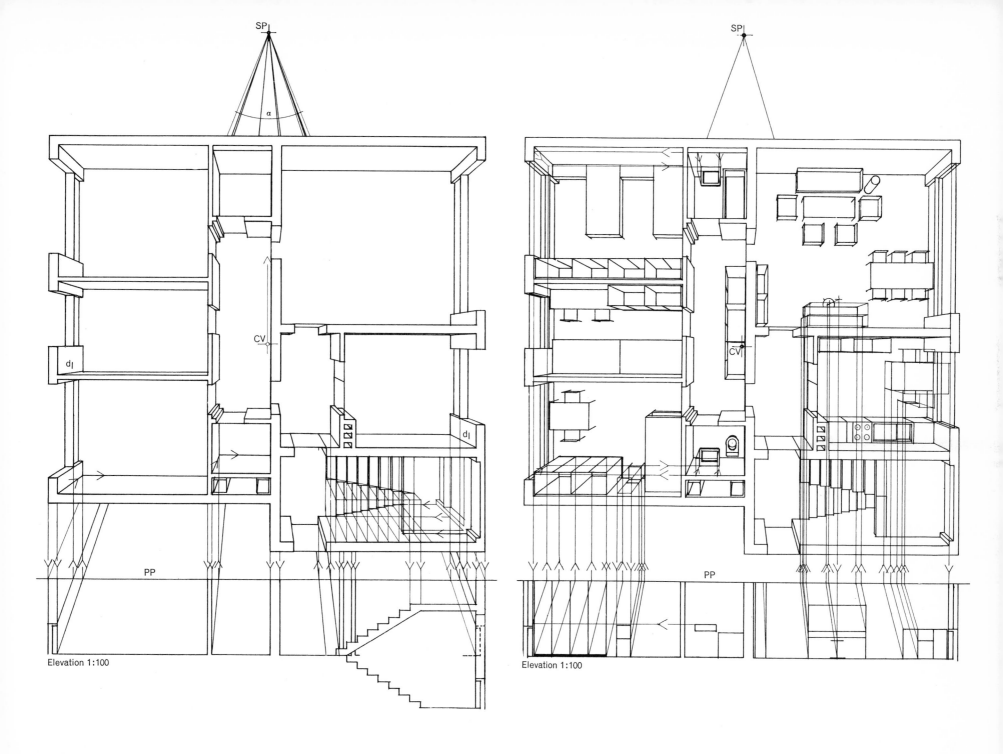

SP

α

CV

d

d

PP

Elevation 1:100

SP

CV

PP

Elevation 1:100

65

Diagonal Bird's-eye View, Constructed using Measuring Points

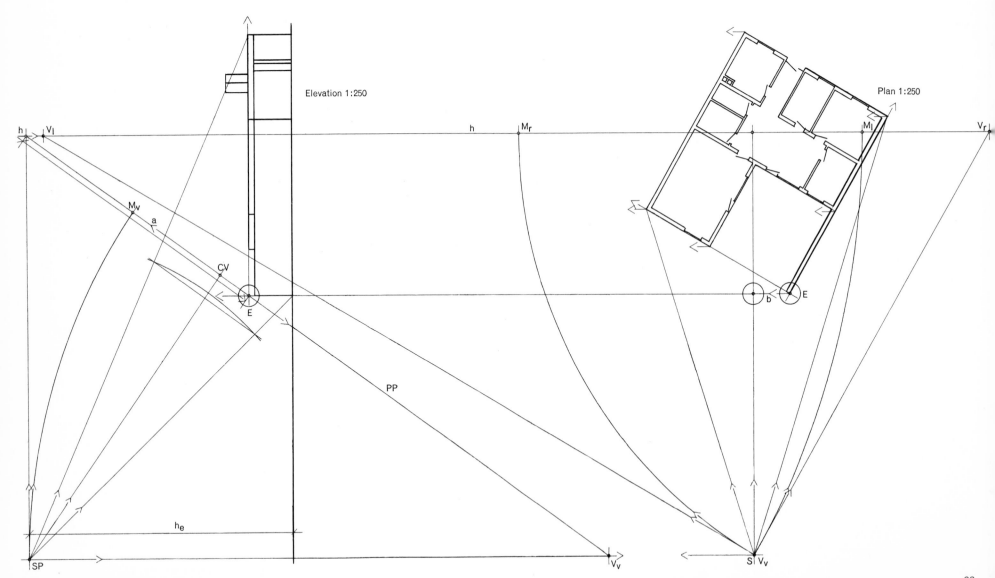

Elevation 1:250

Plan 1:250

h

M_r

V_r

V_l

h

M_v

a

M_l

CV

E

E

b

PP

h_e

V_v

SP

S V_v

For explanation, see opposite page

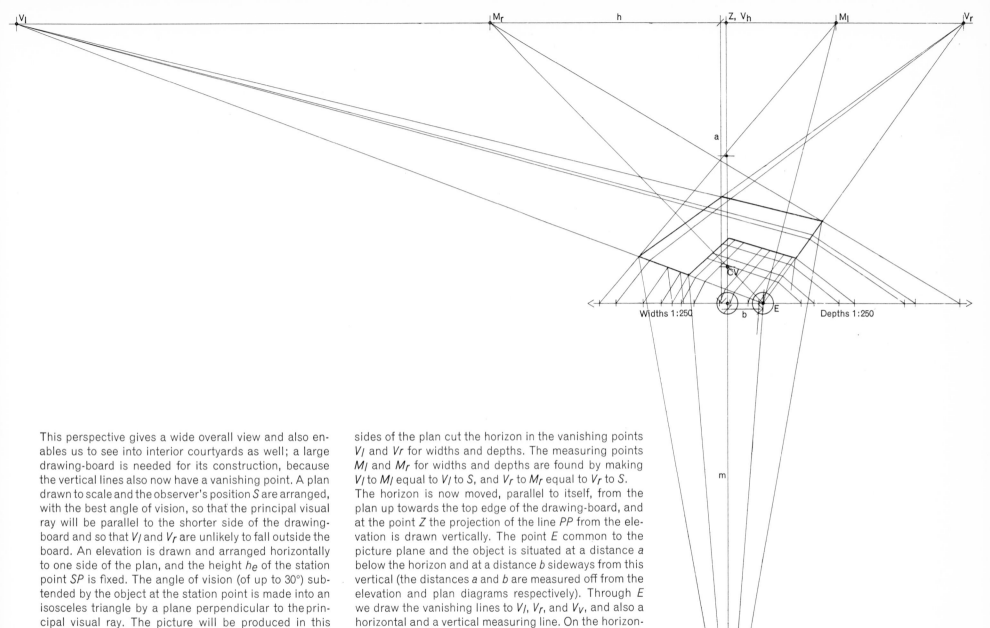

This perspective gives a wide overall view and also enables us to see into interior courtyards as well; a large drawing-board is needed for its construction, because the vertical lines also now have a vanishing point. A plan drawn to scale and the observer's position S are arranged, with the best angle of vision, so that the principal visual ray will be parallel to the shorter side of the drawing-board and so that V_l and V_r are unlikely to fall outside the board. An elevation is drawn and arranged horizontally to one side of the plan, and the height h_e of the station point SP is fixed. The angle of vision (of up to 30°) subtended by the object at the station point is made into an isosceles triangle by a plane perpendicular to the principal visual ray. The picture will be produced in this plane; here it is drawn through the corner point E of the object. Lines drawn through SP parallel to the sides of the elevation cut the picture plane in the horizon h and the vertical vanishing point V_v. The distance between the horizon h and the vertical vanishing point V_v must be less than the depth of the drawing-board. The measuring point M_v for heights is obtained by cutting off along PP an interval V_v to M_v equal to the distance V_v to SP. The horizon is carried back from the elevation into the plan. Lines through the standpoint parallel to the

sides of the plan cut the horizon in the vanishing points V_l and V_r for widths and depths. The measuring points M_l and M_r for widths and depths are found by making V_l to M_l equal to V_l to S, and V_r to M_r equal to V_r to S. The horizon is now moved, parallel to itself, from the plan up towards the top edge of the drawing-board, and at the point Z the projection of the line PP from the elevation is drawn vertically. The point E common to the picture plane and the object is situated at a distance a below the horizon and at a distance b sideways from this vertical (the distances a and b are measured off from the elevation and plan diagrams respectively). Through E we draw the vanishing lines to V_l, V_r, and V_v, and also a horizontal and a vertical measuring line. On the horizontal line we plot (on the same scale as in the plan) towards the left the scale for building widths, and towards the right the scale for building depths. Rays to the horizontal measuring points M_l and M_r cut the vanishing lines to V_l and V_r respectively in the corresponding perspective points. From these points further vanishing lines to V_r and V_l form a perspective plan of the roof, and lines from this to V_v, the vertical vanishing point, form the images of the vertical edges of the object.

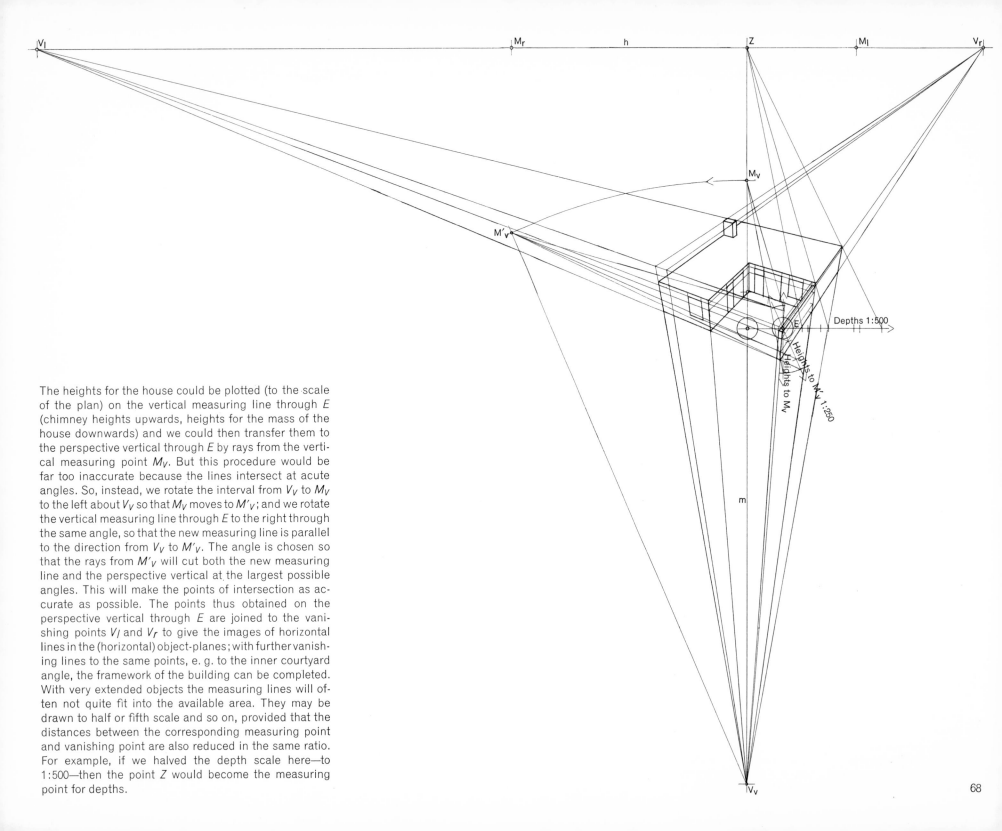

The labels in the figure include:

V_l M_r h Z M_l V_r

M_v

M'_v

E Depths 1:500

Heights to M'_v 1:250

Heights to M_v

m

V_v

The heights for the house could be plotted (to the scale of the plan) on the vertical measuring line through E (chimney heights upwards, heights for the mass of the house downwards) and we could then transfer them to the perspective vertical through E by rays from the vertical measuring point M_v. But this procedure would be far too inaccurate because the lines intersect at acute angles. So, instead, we rotate the interval from V_v to M_v to the left about V_v so that M_v moves to M'_v; and we rotate the vertical measuring line through E to the right through the same angle, so that the new measuring line is parallel to the direction from V_v to M'_v. The angle is chosen so that the rays from M'_v will cut both the new measuring line and the perspective vertical at the largest possible angles. This will make the points of intersection as accurate as possible. The points thus obtained on the perspective vertical through E are joined to the vanishing points V_l and V_r to give the images of horizontal lines in the (horizontal) object-planes; with further vanishing lines to the same points, e. g. to the inner courtyard angle, the framework of the building can be completed. With very extended objects the measuring lines will often not quite fit into the available area. They may be drawn to half or fifth scale and so on, provided that the distances between the corresponding measuring point and vanishing point are also reduced in the same ratio. For example, if we halved the depth scale here—to 1:500—then the point Z would become the measuring point for depths.

68

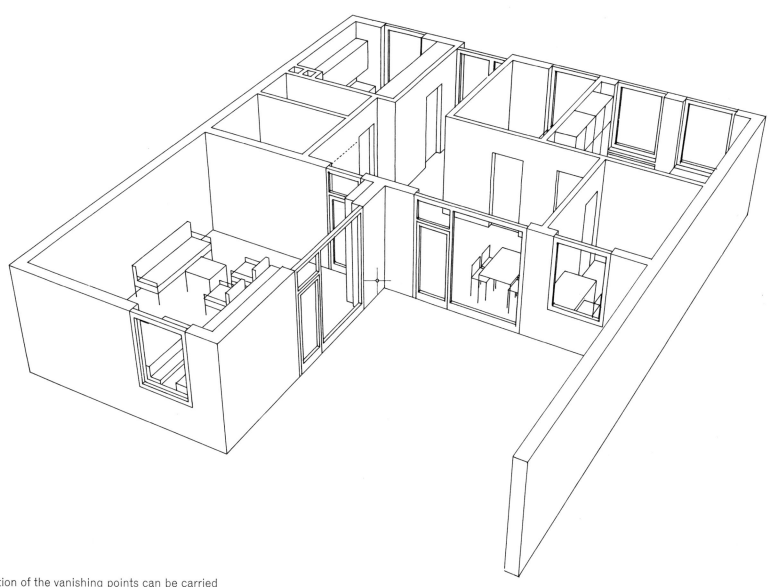

Magnification
The construction of the vanishing points can be carried
out on a small scale, and then the perspective can be
drawn in a larger size; here it has been increased fourfold. The distance between the picture plane and the
station point should be at least 30 cm. (12 in.).

69

Diagonal Worm's-eye View with Outline constructed by Visual Rays

For explanation, see opposite page

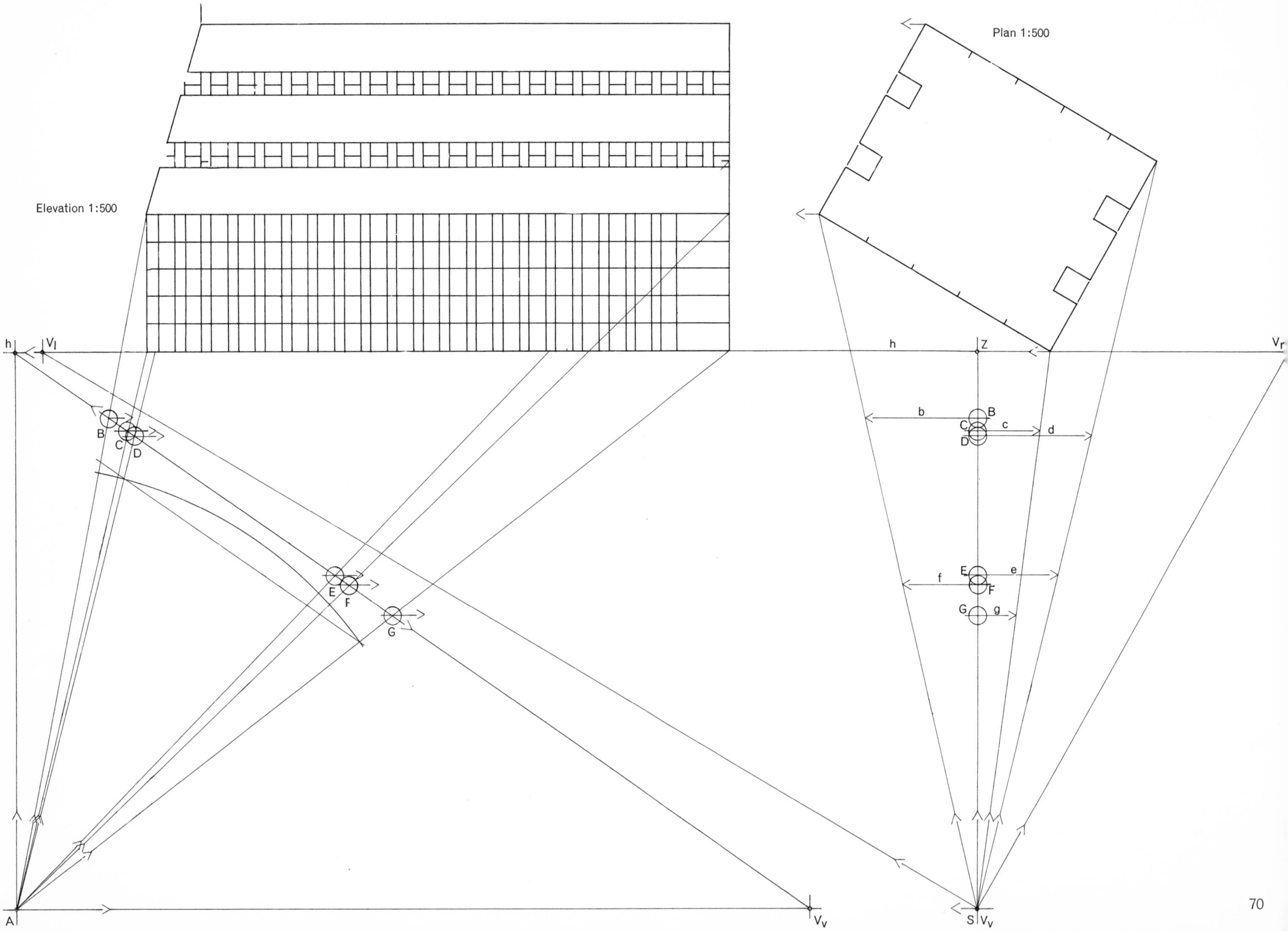

Elevation 1:500

Plan 1:500

Required: Plan and knowledge of the heights.

This perspective could be drawn in exactly the same way as the preceding bird's-eye view was constructed, or the following method may be used instead. The difference is that, after arranging the plan and elevation (it is essential that the distance between the horizon and the vertical vanishing point, h to V_v, should be less than the depth of the board), the images of the most important points of the object are determined by means of visual rays in both diagrams. The transfer from the elevation diagram of the points of intersection $B, C, D, \ldots$ with the picture plane into the plan diagram gives the deviations $b, c, d, \ldots$ in the latter of the image points from the fore-shortened centre-line, Z to V_v, of the picture.

The horizon with V_l and V_r on it is moved down parallel to, and close to, the lower edge of the drawing-board; at the point Z the picture axis m is erected vertically and on it V_v is plotted using the distance (h to V_v) taken from the elevation diagram. The points $B, C, D, \ldots$ are plotted similarly, taking the distance from the elevation diagram. The point L at a sideways distance b from B, the point O at a sideways distance c from C, the point R at a sideways distance d from D, and the point S at a sideways distance g from G, when joined by vanishing lines to the points V_r, V_l, V_v, give the outline of the building. Width and depth scales are plotted from the corner O to the left and right respectively along a horizontal line on arbitrary scales. Lines through the points of subdivision corresponding to the extreme points of the building and through the corresponding image points R and L determine the measuring points M_r and M_l on the horizon line h. From these measuring points the remaining points of subdivision for the building can be determined.

To subdivide the (convergent) perspective verticals, the building heights are plotted (to an arbitrary scale) on a line drawn from the point O in an arbitrary direction. A line parallel to this scale is drawn through the vertical vanishing point V_v. This parallel is cut by the line joining the corner S to the top point H of the arbitrary scale in the measuring point M'_v. Heights can be transferred from the chosen height scale OH on to the edge of the building by rays from M'_v. To obtain greatest accuracy, the direction and scale of this oblique height scale through O must be chosen so that the rays from M'_v to points of the scale will cut the side OS at angles as large as possible. Finally, vanishing lines from these points of intersection to the vanishing points V_l and V_r complete the picture.

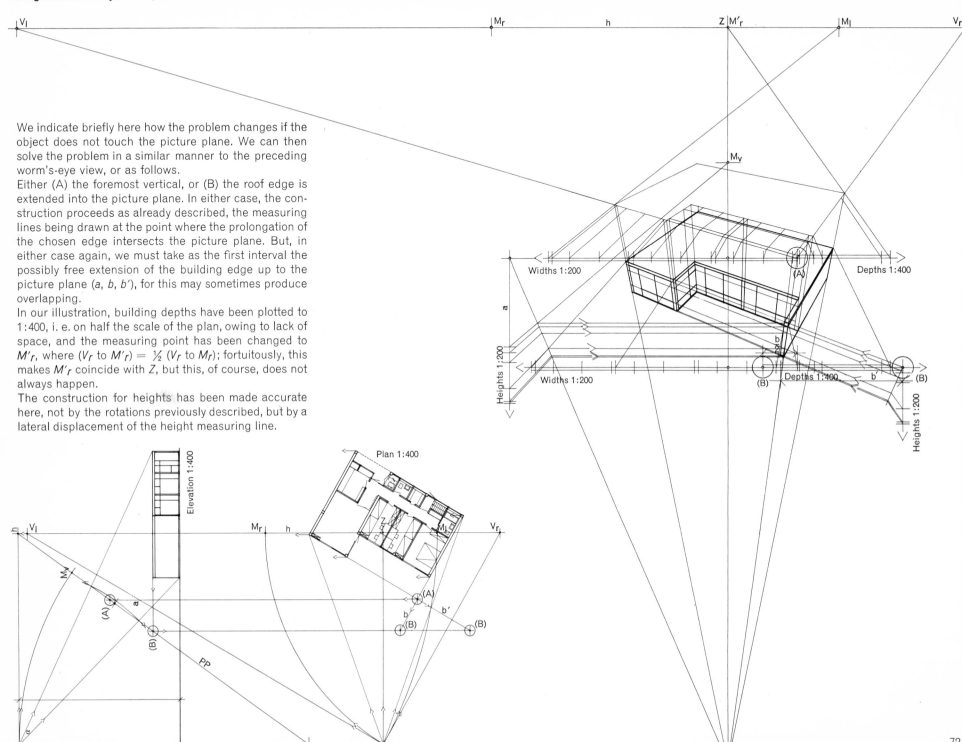

We indicate briefly here how the problem changes if the object does not touch the picture plane. We can then solve the problem in a similar manner to the preceding worm's-eye view, or as follows.

Either (A) the foremost vertical, or (B) the roof edge is extended into the picture plane. In either case, the construction proceeds as already described, the measuring lines being drawn at the point where the prolongation of the chosen edge intersects the picture plane. But, in either case again, we must take as the first interval the possibly free extension of the building edge up to the picture plane (a, b, b'), for this may sometimes produce overlapping.

In our illustration, building depths have been plotted to 1:400, i. e. on half the scale of the plan, owing to lack of space, and the measuring point has been changed to M'_r, where $(V_r$ to $M'_r) = \frac{1}{2} (V_r$ to $M_r)$; fortuitously, this makes M'_r coincide with Z, but this, of course, does not always happen.

The construction for heights has been made accurate here, not by the rotations previously described, but by a lateral displacement of the height measuring line.

Widths 1:200

Depths 1:400

Heights 1:200

Heights 1:200

Widths 1:200

Depths 1:400

Elevation 1:400

Plan 1:400

72

Shadows in Perspectives

If we wish to introduce shadows into a perspective drawing, we have to simplify reality: lamps are regarded as point sources; the sun's rays are taken to be parallel. We do not put into perspective drawings shadows as they would arise from candelabra or rows of windows, because it would be too laborious to do so. There are then six possible types of illumination to be considered:

1. Sun in front of the station point
2. Sun's rays parallel to the picture plane
3. Sun behind the station point
4. Lamp in front of the station point
5. Lamp to the side of the station point
6. Lamp behind the station point

Cases 5 and 6 occur when flash photographs are taken, but are very rarely used in perspective drawings.

Shadows are, in general, constructed as follows:

1. The direction of the light rays, or their vanishing point, is settled either arbitrarily or by specifying angles.

2. We imagine a plane which contains the light ray and which cuts the surface on which the shadow is to be cast. The outline formed by the intersection of the plane with the surface is constructed.

3. Where the light ray cuts the outline formed by the intersection of the plane with the surface on which the shadow is cast we find the shadow of the given point. Sometimes it does not exist!

Cube illuminated by three lamps

73

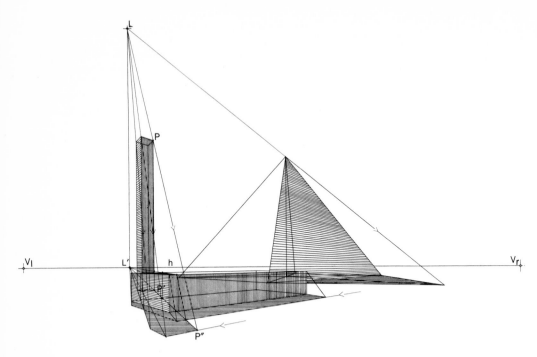

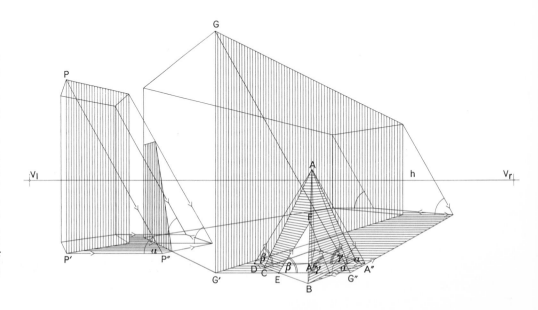

Sunlight from in front

The sun's rays, parallel to one another and incident on the picture plane from in front, have in the perspective a vanishing point L. It is situated at the point where the sun's ray which passes through the station point cuts the picture plane. It is always above the horizon, and may be put in arbitrarily; it should not, however, be too close to the horizon, otherwise the shadows will be too long. Vertically below L on the horizon we have the point L', which may be called the sub-solar point. L' is the vanishing point of the plan projections of all the sun's rays, that is to say, it is also the vanishing point of the shadows on horizontal planes of the vertical edges of the object. The points L, L' and a light ray through an object point P determine a vertical plane which cuts all the surfaces on which shadows may be cast. It intersects the ground plane along the plan projection of the light ray (this plan projection running from the vanishing point L' to the vertical projection P' of the point P); it intersects vertical walls in a vertical line running upwards from their bottom edge; it intersects the upper rectangle plane (on the object) through P in a line which is again directed towards L'. If there is a shadow point, it is the point P'' where the light ray meets the surface on which the shadow is being cast. If P lies on the line LL' the construction just described is impossible. But we can usually manage, because the shadow of some other point is constructible and the vanishing point of the shadow boundaries is known. We note also that the shadows of straight lines on to planes which are parallel to them are themselves parallel to the lines casting the shadows.

Sunlight from the side

If the sun's rays are parallel to the picture plane, they also remain parallel in the perspective. The auxiliary figure needed for constructing the shadows will also not be distorted but only changed in size. This auxiliary figure consists, for each point P, of the light ray at the prescribed angle α, of the vertical PP', and of either a horizontal ground line or of a section through the part of an encountered object up to the point P'' where the light ray appears.

For example, the shadow of the vertical edge GG' of the right-hand rectangular block is thrown partly on to the ground and partly on to the face ABC of the small pyramid. The direction of the shadow EF on the face ABC is found from a parallel direction through the top of the pyramid which we obtain by cutting the illuminated face by a cross-section parallel to the picture plane through the pyramid axis AA'. In detail, the edge CB produced goes through the vanishing point V_l; AA' is the altitude of the pyramid; A'D is drawn parallel to h to intersect CB produced at D. Hence the direction AD is determined. The shadow of GG' runs along the ground from G to E, where it meets the face ABC of the pyramid. Through E we draw EF parallel to AD. Then the part ABEF of the pyramid face is in shadow and the triangle CEF is illuminated.

On a vertical surface the shadows of all vertical edges would be vertical.

Lines and their shadows on surfaces parallel to them have the same vanishing points or are parallel to one another.

74

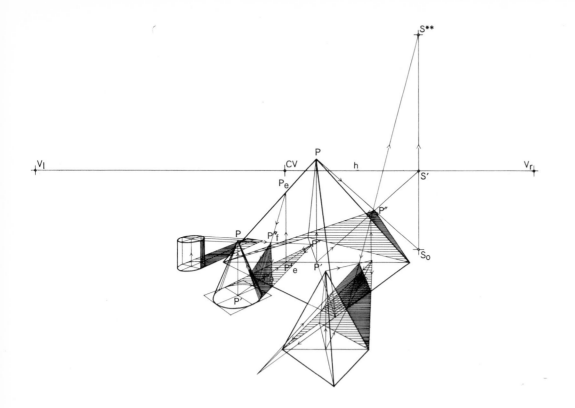

Sunlight from behind

The vanishing point S_o for the sun's rays lies below the horizon somewhere to that side to which the shadows are to fall. Shadows cast by vertical lines on to horizontal planes run towards S', the foot of the perpendicular from S_o on to the horizon h. To determine the shadow of a point P, a light ray is drawn from P to S_o; the perspective plan of this light ray, from P' to S', cuts the light ray PS_o in the required shadow point P''.

The shadow cast by a cone or pyramid on to horizontal planes is found by constructing the shadow point of the vertex and then drawing tangents from this point to the perspective plan of the object. These tangents are the edges of the shadow cast by the object on to the ground (or horizontal plane) and the lines joining the points of contact of the tangents to the vertex of the body mark the limit of the body's shadow on itself. If the shadow point of the vertex of the pyramid falls inside the perspective plan of the pyramid, then the latter has no shadow.

To obtain the shadows cast by the nearer pyramids on the farther pyramid, we proceed thus. Corresponding to the light ray through the vertex of a (nearer) pyramid, we make a vertical section through that pyramid. The plan of the light ray will intersect a bottom edge of the farther pyramid in a point, e. g. P_b in our diagram, and will also intersect the plan of one of the sloping edges of the farther pyramid in a point, the point P'_e in our case. At P'_e we erect the perpendicular upwards to meet the sloping edge in P_e and then join P_e and P_b. The point P''_f where $P_e P_b$ intersects the light ray PS_o is the shadow point of P on the sloping face of the farther pyramid. The shadow cast on the sloping face can now easily be drawn.

Notice that the extension of a join like $P_b P_e$ will go through some point S^* on the vertical line $S_o S$ and that this point S^* is the vanishing point for all lines parallel to $P_b P_e$ on that side of the farther pyramid. (For lack of space S^* is not shown in our diagram, but a similar point S^{**} is.)

A lamp in the picture

If the light source is in front of the observer, then its centre L will appear in the perspective. To determine the shadow cast by one object on another, e. g. the shadow of an edge cast on to a plane, we need more than the perspective images of the light rays alone. We have to think of an auxiliary plane associated with each light ray, whose intersection with the object is drawn perspectively, and which, if it is cut by the light ray, will determine the shadow point. The simplest auxiliary planes for the construction of the boundary of the illumination on a plane are planes which are actually perpendicular to the illuminated plane and which rotate, like a wind-vane as it were, about the perpendicular from the light point L on to the wall, ceiling, or ground surface concerned. The intersection of an auxiliary plane through the point P, for instance, runs through the foot L' of the perpendicular from the light point L and through the foot P' of the perpendicular from P, the point casting the shadow. This line of intersection is the shadow cast on the ground plane by a vertical through P, and where it is met by the light ray through P is the shadow point P''. (Remember that each particular plane has its own particular point L', the foot of the perpendicular from L on to that plane.)

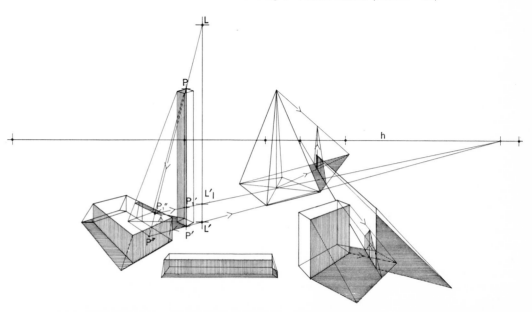

Lamplight from the Side

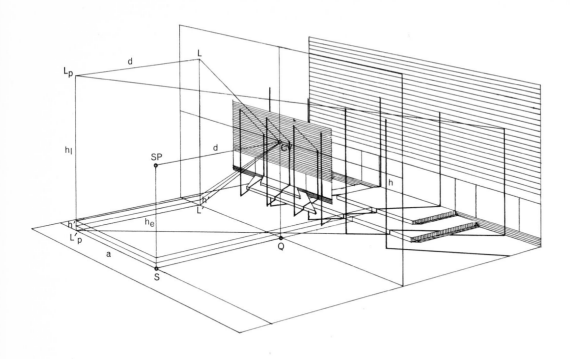

The space configuration

The diagram shows in perspective the space configuration when shadows are being cast by a lamp L_p situated at a distance a to one side of the standpoint S. We are given the lamp L_p at a height h_l, the foot L'_p of the perpendicular from L_p, the station point SP at a height h_e above S, all four points being at a distance d from the picture plane; the corresponding points in the drawing, L, L', CV, and Q, are obtained by horizontal parallel projection perpendicular to the picture plane. In the perspective drawing, then, the images of all light rays will be parallel to SP-L_p, i.e. to CV-L, and the images of the shadows cast by vertical lines on to a plane parallel to the ground will be parallel to the line SP-L'_p, i.e. to CV-L', where the actual position of the points L'_p and L' depends on the height h' of the horizontal plane in question.

All rays emanating from any particular point in the plane through the station point parallel to the picture plane will appear in the perspective drawing as a family of parallel lines. This plane is known as the vanishing plane.

The construction

The perspective is drawn and the centre of vision CV and the points L, L' are plotted. They are situated at a distance a (taken from the plan) to one side of CV. L' is a distance equal to the height of eye, h_e, below the horizon, and L is at a distance equal to the height of the lamp, h_l, above L', these distances being plotted on the same scale as that of the elevation. Through an image point P a light ray is drawn parallel to the line L-CV, and through the foot of the perpendicular from P on to ground level the plan projection of the light ray is drawn parallel to the line L'-CV. Where the light ray PP'' intersects its plan projection $P'P''$ is the required shadow point P''. Each plane on to which a shadow is cast has its own particular point P' = foot of the perpendicular from P and also its own direction for light rays.

The shadows cast by straight lines on to planes parallel to these lines are either parallel to the perspective images of the original (shadow-casting) lines or they have a common vanishing point with them.

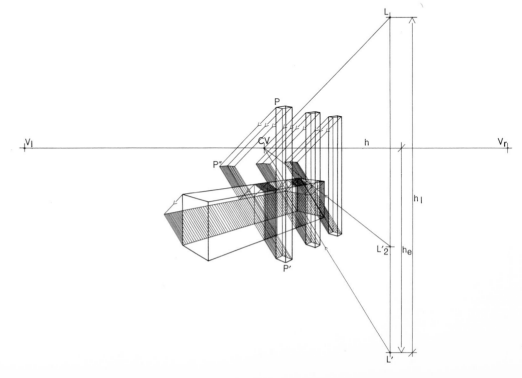

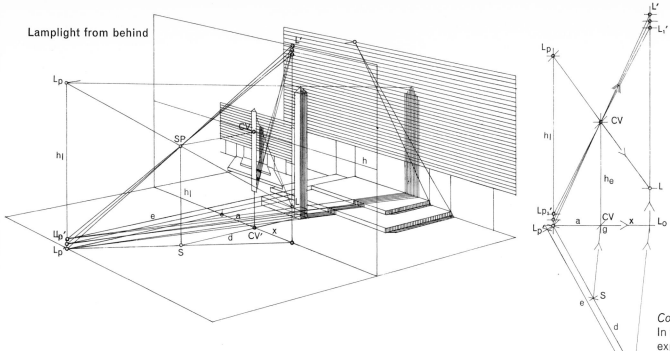

Lamplight from behind

The space configuration

This shows how the necessary vanishing points are found. Let the object, picture plane, station point SP, standpoint S, light point Lp, the foot Lp' of the perpendicular from Lp on to the ground and the corresponding points for the other parallel planes (including possibly the ceiling) all be given. The vanishing point L for light rays is obtained as the point where the line Lp-SP produced cuts the picture plane. The vanishing point L' for the plan projections of light rays is obtained as the point where the line $L'p$-SP cuts the picture plane; and similarly for the vanishing point of their projections on to other parallel planes, including the ceiling.

The position of the points L and L, in the picture plane can be determined as shown in the diagram. At a distance h_e below CV are the point CV' and the ground line g. Lp' is at a horizontal distance a from CV', Lp at a height h_l vertically above Lp'. The distance e is marked off from Lp' with the subdivision S, and with parallel rays drawn on g in such a way that S falls on CV'. The projection of the free end of e on g then determines the length x and the point L^o. L and L' lie on the perpendicular through L^o, where this meets the rays from Lp and Lp' through CV.

The vanishing point for the projections of light rays on to any of the walls would be obtained from the extension of the wall, the foot of the perpendicular from Lp on to the wall, and rays from the foot of the perpendicular from SP on to the picture plane.

Construction

In the example shown the points L and L' are first fixed as explained above. The shadow P'' of a point P is then obtained as the point of intersection of the straight lines PL and $P'L'$.

To find the shadow of PP' on the other block, we erect a vertical at the point of intersection of the line $P'L'$ with the plan rectangle of the box and find its point of intersection with the upper edge of the block. Where the line joining the points of intersection of the ceiling edge, produced, cuts the vertical LL' is the vanishing point L_2' of all shadows of verticals on the upper surface of the block. But L_2' can also be determined in another way: $L'L$ stands in the same relationship to $L'L_2'$ as the height of the lamp h_l to the height of the block h_b. This proportion can be transferred to $L'L$ by the construction given on p. 14 (left, above).

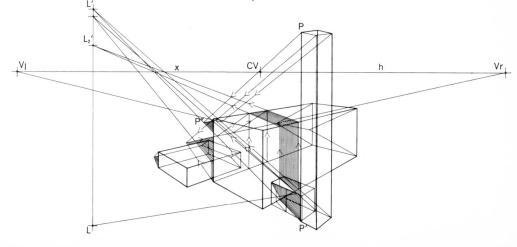

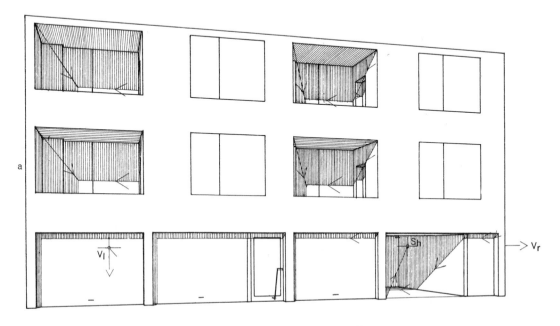

Example 1

The perspective has been drawn using the plan and visual rays construction; the side *a* is on the scale 1:100. The sun's rays run towards the arbitrarily chosen point S_o; the shadows cast by vertical edges on to the horizontal ground run towards the point S_h, vertically above S_o on the horizon *h*; the shadows of horizontal edges on to transverse walls run towards S_l, vertically below V_l on the straight line from V_r through S_o. The shadows cast by lines on to walls parallel to these lines run towards the same vanishing point as the lines themselves. The construction presents no difficulties when the vanishing points are known.

Example 2 (diagram opposite)

The house has been drawn using a perspective ground plan which itself has been constructed by means of a measuring line and the measuring and vanishing points. The edge *a* of the house lies in the picture plane. The sun's rays run towards the arbitrarily chosen point S_o. The plan projection of the light rays for the construction of shadows by vertical edges on to the horizontal plane go through S_h, vertically above S_o on the horizon *h*. The position of shadow points on the façade is determined by lines drawn in the perspective ground plan towards S_h. Where the verticals from these points cut the corresponding light rays in the picture the corresponding shadow points are situated.

The shadows cast on the façade by edges projecting perpendicularly outward from the façade point towards the point S_r which is situated vertically below V_r on the line through V_l and S_o. The shadows cast by horizontal longitudinal edges on to transverse walls standing out perpendicular to the façade point towards S_l, which is situated vertically below V_l on the straight line through V_r and S_o.

78

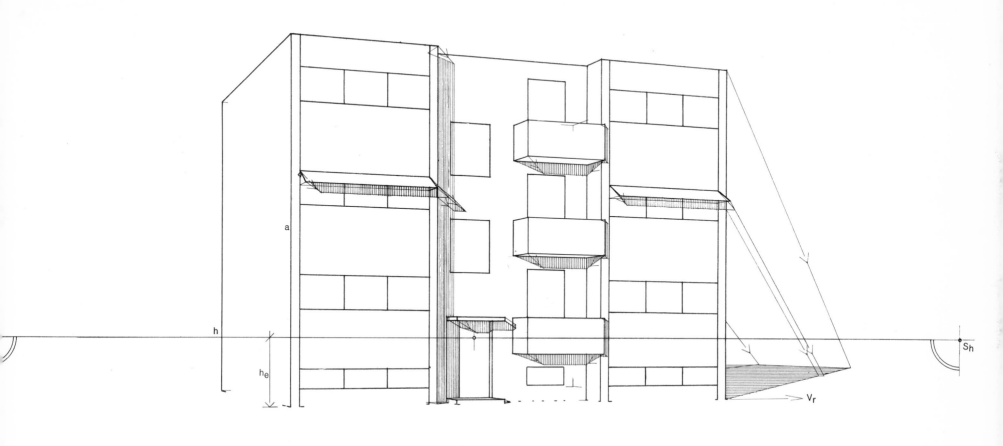
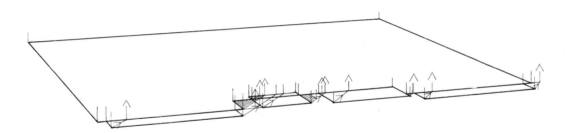

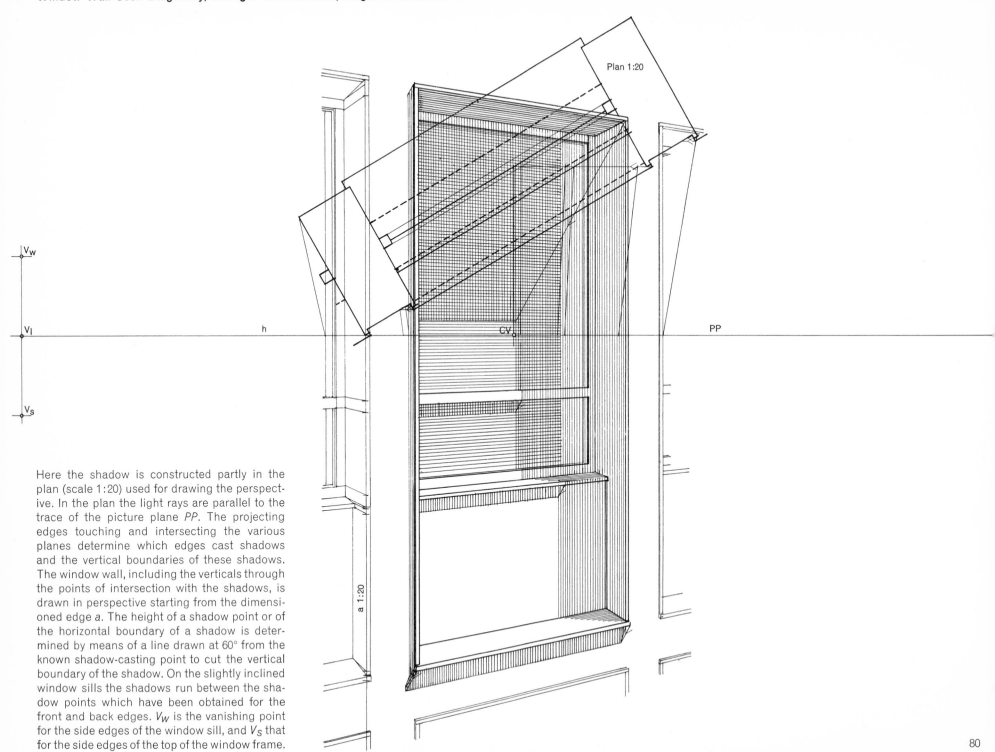

Plan 1:20

V_W

V_l h   CV   PP

V_S

a 1:20

Here the shadow is constructed partly in the plan (scale 1:20) used for drawing the perspective. In the plan the light rays are parallel to the trace of the picture plane *PP*. The projecting edges touching and intersecting the various planes determine which edges cast shadows and the vertical boundaries of these shadows. The window wall, including the verticals through the points of intersection with the shadows, is drawn in perspective starting from the dimensioned edge *a*. The height of a shadow point or of the horizontal boundary of a shadow is determined by means of a line drawn at 60° from the known shadow-casting point to cut the vertical boundary of the shadow. On the slightly inclined window sills the shadows run between the shadow points which have been obtained for the front and back edges. V_W is the vanishing point for the side edges of the window sill, and V_S that for the side edges of the top of the window frame.

80

A Tube in Sunlight; Shadows in the Tube and on the Ground

To construct the shadow in the tube we think of auxiliary planes containing the light rays and intersecting the tube along its generators, i. e. along lines such as m. These auxiliary planes cut the plane across the mouth of the tube in straight lines parallel to the line joining the vanishing point for the sun's rays to the centre of vision, the line S_O-CV. Thus for the point P we obtain the point P' by drawing PP' parallel to S_O-CV, and the generator m by joining P' to CV. The shadow point P'' corresponding to P is then the point of intersection of the line PS_O with m. A perpendicular to S_O-CV through the centre O of the mouth of the tube intersects the circumference in the points A and B, which mark the ends of the shadow thrown by the tube on itself. At these points the sun's rays are tangential; from A and B the edge of the shadow on the outside of the tube runs along the generators.

The shadow cast by the tube on the ground has an elliptical boundary for the parts cast by the free ends of the tube and straight-line boundaries for the parts arising from the generators of the tube. The two ellipses and the straight lines join smoothly without corners at the points A'', B'', C'', D''. Since the construction of shadows cast on the ground has already been described, we merely indicate it in the figure here.

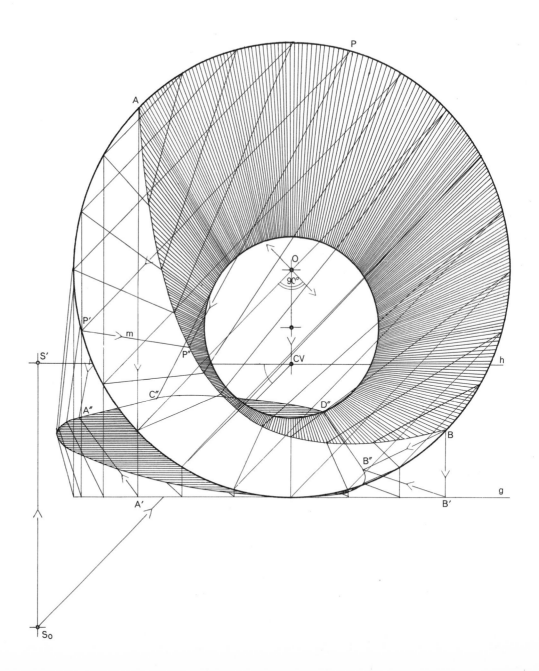

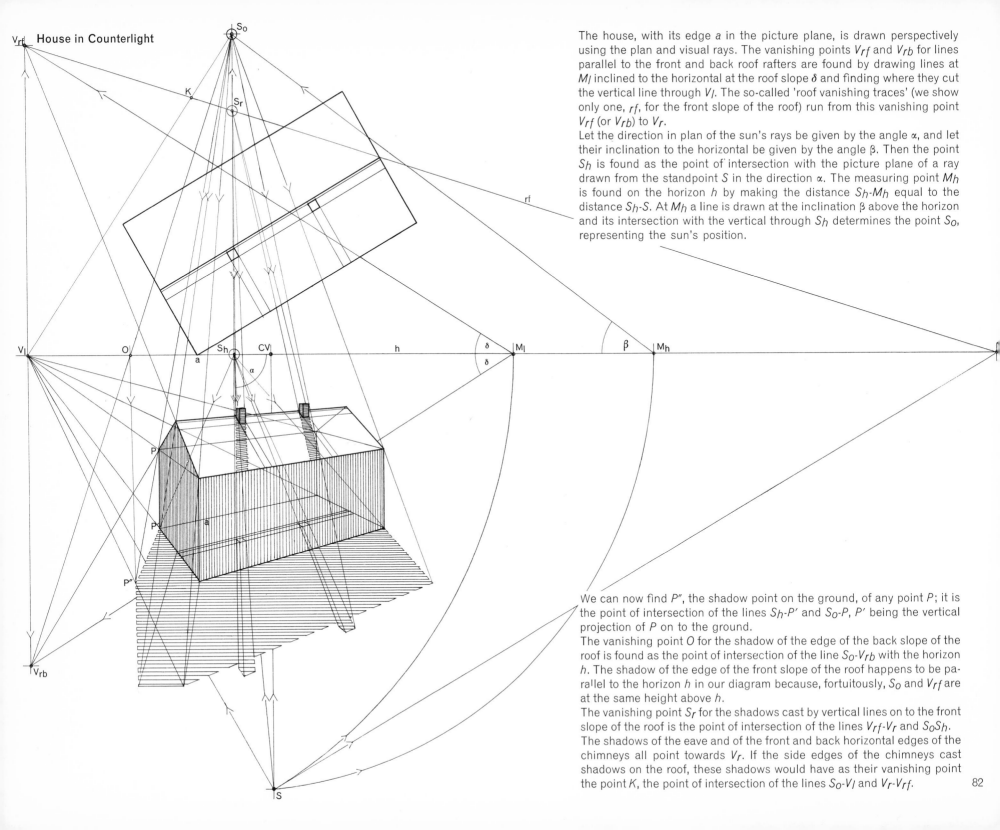

House in Counterlight

The house, with its edge *a* in the picture plane, is drawn perspectively using the plan and visual rays. The vanishing points V_{rf} and V_{rb} for lines parallel to the front and back roof rafters are found by drawing lines at M_l inclined to the horizontal at the roof slope δ and finding where they cut the vertical line through V_l. The so-called 'roof vanishing traces' (we show only one, *rf*, for the front slope of the roof) run from this vanishing point V_{rf} (or V_{rb}) to V_r.

Let the direction in plan of the sun's rays be given by the angle α, and let their inclination to the horizontal be given by the angle β. Then the point S_h is found as the point of intersection with the picture plane of a ray drawn from the standpoint S in the direction α. The measuring point M_h is found on the horizon *h* by making the distance S_h-M_h equal to the distance S_h-S. At M_h a line is drawn at the inclination β above the horizon and its intersection with the vertical through S_h determines the point S_o, representing the sun's position.

We can now find P'', the shadow point on the ground, of any point P; it is the point of intersection of the lines S_h-P' and S_o-P, P' being the vertical projection of P on to the ground.

The vanishing point O for the shadow of the edge of the back slope of the roof is found as the point of intersection of the line S_o-V_{rb} with the horizon *h*. The shadow of the edge of the front slope of the roof happens to be parallel to the horizon *h* in our diagram because, fortuitously, S_o and V_{rf} are at the same height above *h*.

The vanishing point S_r for the shadows cast by vertical lines on to the front slope of the roof is the point of intersection of the lines V_{rf}-V_r and S_oS_h.

The shadows of the eave and of the front and back horizontal edges of the chimneys all point towards V_r. If the side edges of the chimneys cast shadows on the roof, these shadows would have as their vanishing point the point K, the point of intersection of the lines S_o-V_l and V_r-V_{rf}.

82

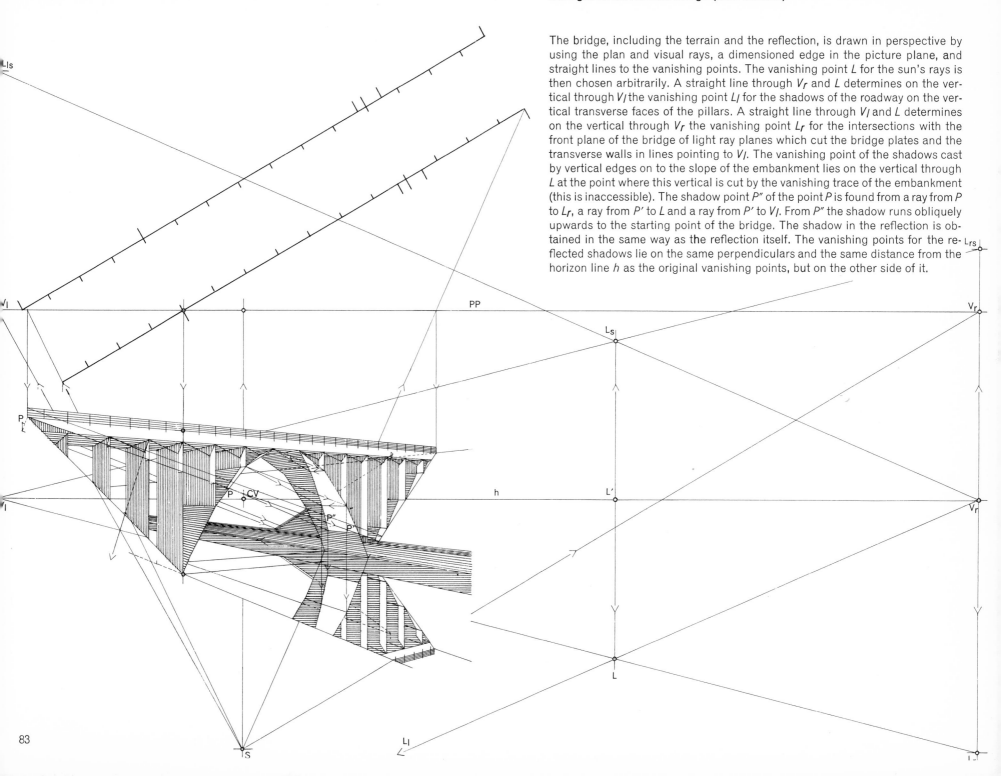

Sunlight on an Arched Bridge (after Maillart)

The bridge, including the terrain and the reflection, is drawn in perspective by using the plan and visual rays, a dimensioned edge in the picture plane, and straight lines to the vanishing points. The vanishing point L for the sun's rays is then chosen arbitrarily. A straight line through V_r and L determines on the vertical through V_l the vanishing point L_l for the shadows of the roadway on the vertical transverse faces of the pillars. A straight line through V_l and L determines on the vertical through V_r the vanishing point L_r for the intersections with the front plane of the bridge of light ray planes which cut the bridge plates and the transverse walls in lines pointing to V_l. The vanishing point of the shadows cast by vertical edges on to the slope of the embankment lies on the vertical through L at the point where this vertical is cut by the vanishing trace of the embankment (this is inaccessible). The shadow point P'' of the point P is found from a ray from P to L_r, a ray from P' to L and a ray from P' to V_l. From P'' the shadow runs obliquely upwards to the starting point of the bridge. The shadow in the reflection is obtained in the same way as the reflection itself. The vanishing points for the reflected shadows lie on the same perpendiculars and the same distance from the horizon line h as the original vanishing points, but on the other side of it.

Staircase seen frontally, Sunlight from behind the Observer

10 steps 15/30 cm. (6/12 in.) = slope of 1:2.

The perspective is constructed by means of depth-lines starting from two edges dimensioned for heights on the scale 1:33.3, rays from two depth-measuring edges on the scale 1:66.6 to the half-distance points and straight lines to the vanishing point V_S for the staircase.

The sun point S_O is chosen arbitrarily. Then the shadows cast by verticals on to horizontal planes run towards S_h, vertically above S_O on the horizon h. The shadow cast by a vertical on a plane inclined at the slope of the stairs, for example, the plane through the front edges of the steps, runs towards the point S_S, which is vertically above S_O and on the same level as V_S. The shadow cast by a vertical on to vertical surfaces is vertical. The shadow cast by a depth-line on to planes containing the depth-lines runs towards the centre of vision, CV. The shadow cast by a depth-line on to a plane inclined at the slope of the stairs runs towards the point S_W (inaccessible in our diagram), which is the point of intersection of the line S_O-CV with the vanishing trace s through V_S and S_S. The shadow cast by a depth-line on to a vertical, transverse plane is parallel to the line S_O-CV. The shadow of a line parallel to the slope of the stairs, for example, the sloping part of the hand-rail, runs on a horizontal plane towards S_g, (the point of intersection of the line S_O-V_S with the horizon h), on the plane through the front edges of the steps and on the vertical side wall (parallel to the steps) towards V_S, and on the vertical transverse wall it is parallel to the line S_O-V_S. The shadow cast by a horizontal transverse line on to the vertical side wall goes through S_t, which is vertically below CV on the level of S_O. The construction proceeds bit by bit from the front of the picture towards the back.

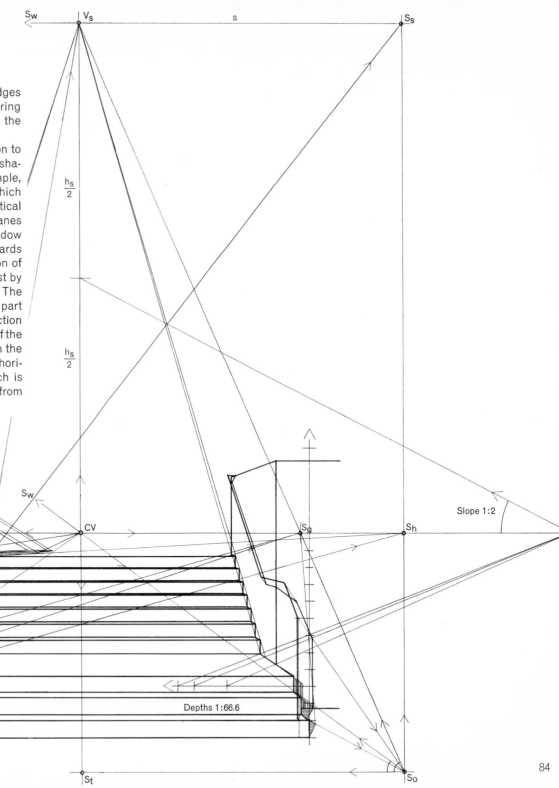

S_W V_S s S_S

$\frac{h_s}{2}$

$\frac{h_s}{2}$

Slope 1:2

S_W

$\frac{D}{2}$ h CV S_g S_h

Heights 1:33.3

Depths 1:66.6

S_t S_O

84

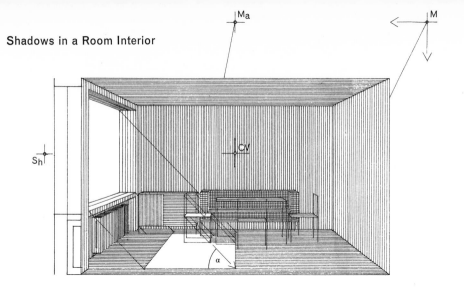

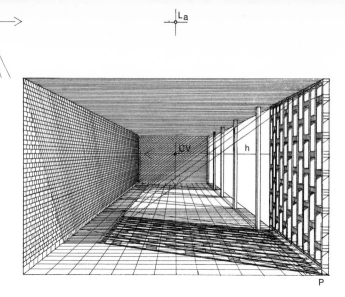

1. Living-room seen frontally, sunlight from the side
All the light rays have the same inclination α; the plan projections of the light rays—that is to say, all the shadows of vertical edges cast on the ground—run horizontally. Shadows of depth-lines are again depth-lines. In determining the size of the patch of light on the ground, at the top of the window frame it is the outer edge which counts and at the bottom of the window the inner edge.

2. Waiting-hall seen frontally, sunlight from behind the observer
The light rays run to the arbitrarily chosen point S_O. Shadows cast by vertical edges on the ground run from the perspective plan point P to S_h, the point vertically above S_O on the horizon h. The shadows cast by horizontal transverse lines on to the side wall run towards S_a, situated vertically below CV on the same horizontal level as S_O. The shadow cast by the overhang on to the back wall and the edges of the shadows in the honeycomb structure are parallel to the line CV-S_O.

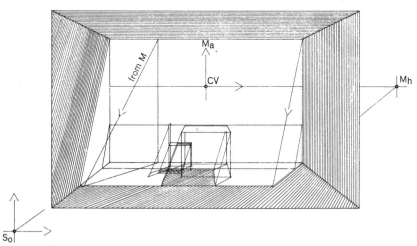

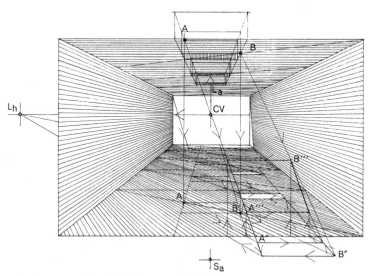

3. Work-room seen frontally, moonlight from in front of the observer
The light rays come from the arbitrarily chosen point M. The shadows cast by vertical edges on to the ground (i. e. the plan projections of light rays) run towards M_h; the shadows cast by horizontal transverse lines on to the side walls run towards M_a. Here M_h lies vertically below M on the horizon, and M_a lies vertically above CV on the picture axis at the same horizontal level as M.

4. Passage with skylights, seen frontally
The light comes from the point L. We need to construct, by drawing the light rays and the plan projections of the light rays (which are directed towards L_h), the shadow points for only two boundary points A and B of one of the skylights. The boundaries of the other shadows can then be found using only depth-lines, plan lines and verticals.

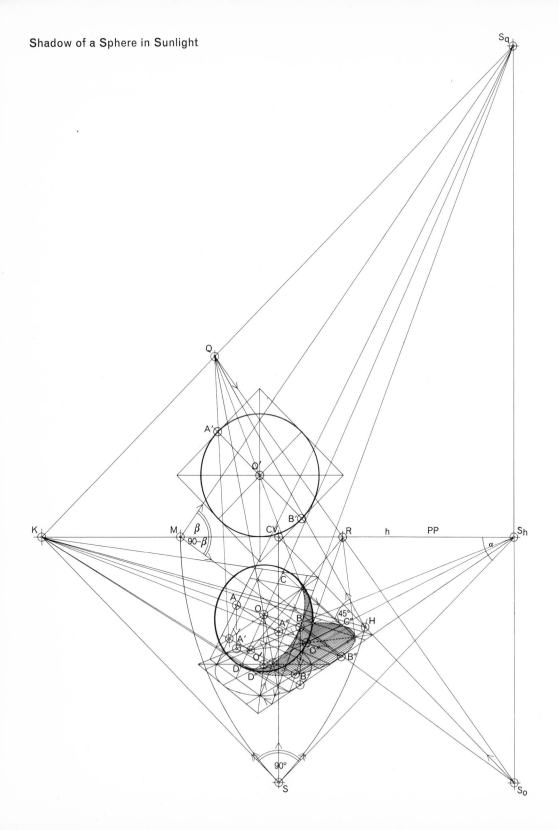

We draw the picture of the sphere, including its perspective plan (see page 110). Then the diameter *AOB* and its plan projection *A'O'B'*, both perpendicular to the plan direction α of the light rays, are drawn in the perspective. Lines through the standpoint *S* parallel and perpendicular to this direction α determine the vanishing points *K* and *Sh* on the picture plane trace (which here is the horizon *h*). A circle about *Sh* through *S* fixes the measuring point *M* on *h*. Through *M* a ray is plotted at the true elevation β of the light rays, and another one at right angles to it; these cut the vertical through *Sh* in the vanishing point *So* for the sun's rays and in the point *Sq* respectively. The boundary of the shadow of the sphere on itself is a great circle, the intersection of the sphere by a plane perpendicular to the sun's rays and containing the diameter *AOB*. Straight lines from *A, O, B* to *Sq* form two sides and an axis of the square which circumscribes the circle of intersection. Straight lines from *A', O', B'* to *Sh* form two sides and an axis of the rectangle which circumscribes the ellipse that forms the boundary of the shadow cast on the ground by the sphere. Straight lines from *A, O, B* to *So* cut the lines to *Sh* which we have just mentioned in the points *A", O", B"* respectively; these are the shadow points of *A, O, B*, and so they determine the second axis of the rectangle circumscribing the ellipse. *Q*, the vanishing point of one of the diagonals of the square mentioned above, and *R*, the vanishing point of one of the diagonals of the rectangle just mentioned, are determined as follows.

A perpendicular from *So* on to *KSq* and a circle about *K* through *S* define the point *H*. A line inclined at 45° to *HK* is plotted at *H* to intersect *KSq* in the point *Q*. The straight line *QSo* intersects the horizon in *R*.

Now, the line *OQ* cuts the lines *ASq* and *BSq* in points which determine the perspective length of the circumscribing square, which may be completed by joining these points of intersection to *K*. Similarly, the line *O"R* cuts the lines *A"Sh* and *B"Sh* in points which determine the length of the circumscribing rectangle, which, again, may be completed by joining these points of intersection to *K*. The boundaries of the shadows on the sphere itself and on the ground both appear as ellipses. The first goes through the points *A, B, C, D* and is contained in the perspective square; the second goes through *A", B", C", D"* and is contained in the perspective rectangle. Intermediate points and tangents, if needed, can easily be produced.

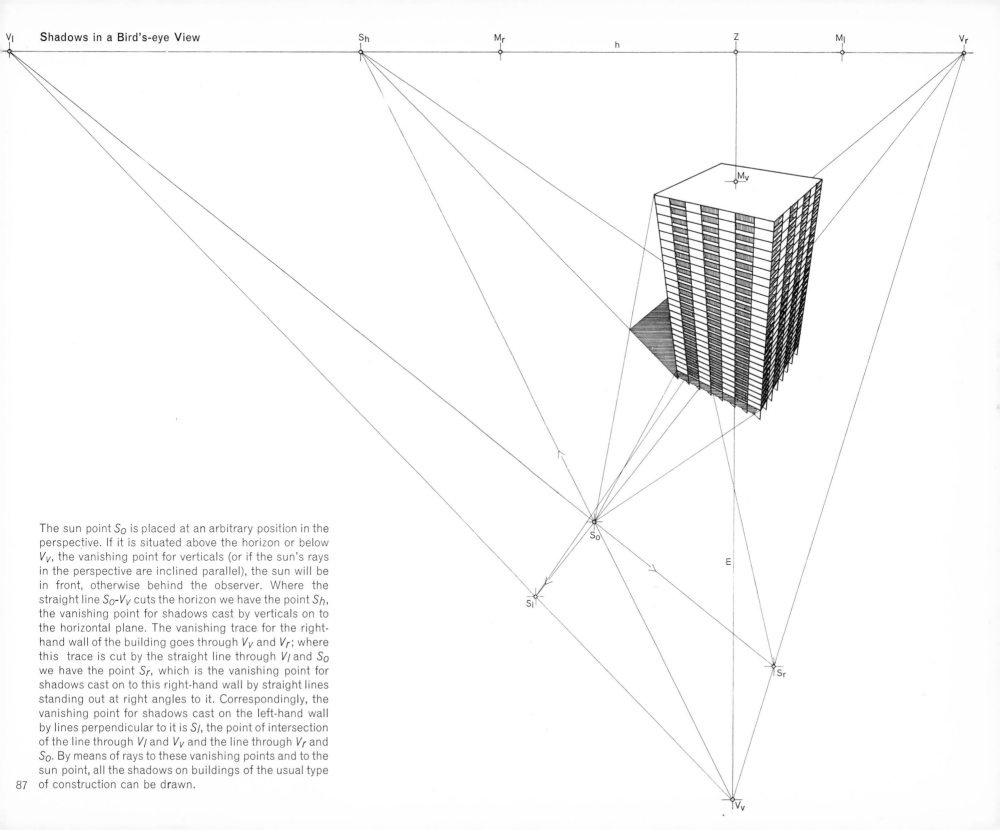

V_l S_h M_r h Z M_l V_r

M_v

S_o

S_l

E

S_r

V_v

The sun point S_o is placed at an arbitrary position in the perspective. If it is situated above the horizon or below V_v, the vanishing point for verticals (or if the sun's rays in the perspective are inclined parallel), the sun will be in front, otherwise behind the observer. Where the straight line S_o-V_v cuts the horizon we have the point S_h, the vanishing point for shadows cast by verticals on to the horizontal plane. The vanishing trace for the right-hand wall of the building goes through V_v and V_r; where this trace is cut by the straight line through V_l and S_o we have the point S_r, which is the vanishing point for shadows cast on to this right-hand wall by straight lines standing out at right angles to it. Correspondingly, the vanishing point for shadows cast on the left-hand wall by lines perpendicular to it is S_l, the point of intersection of the line through V_l and V_v and the line through V_r and S_o. By means of rays to these vanishing points and to the sun point, all the shadows on buildings of the usual type of construction can be drawn.

87

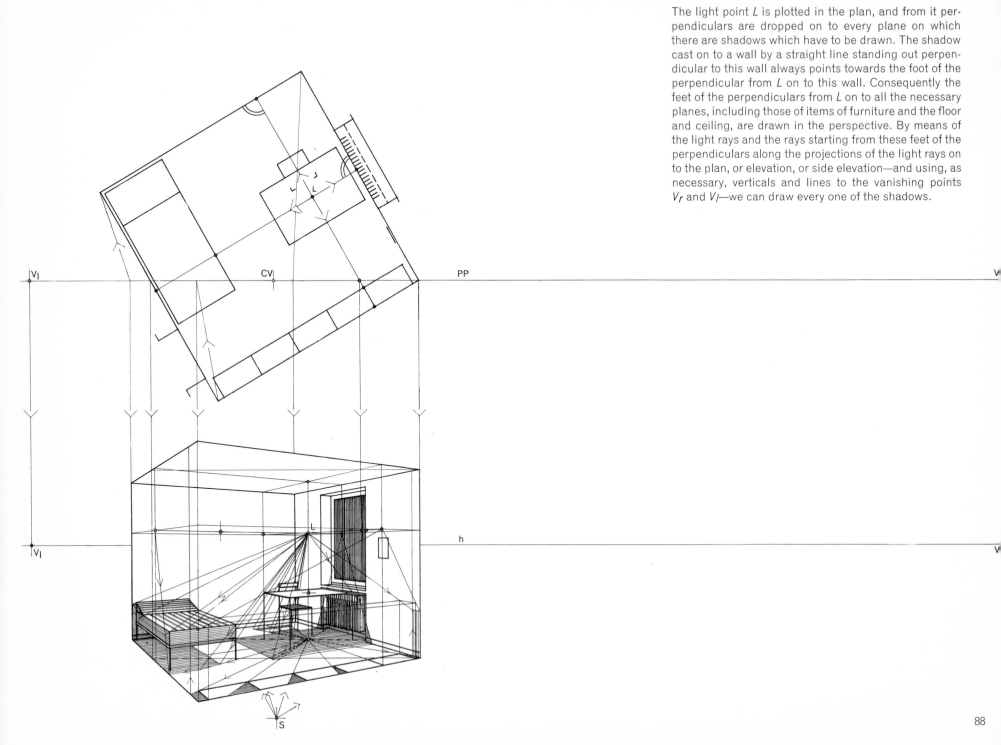

The light point *L* is plotted in the plan, and from it perpendiculars are dropped on to every plane on which there are shadows which have to be drawn. The shadow cast on to a wall by a straight line standing out perpendicular to this wall always points towards the foot of the perpendicular from *L* on to this wall. Consequently the feet of the perpendiculars from *L* on to all the necessary planes, including those of items of furniture and the floor and ceiling, are drawn in the perspective. By means of the light rays and the rays starting from these feet of the perpendiculars along the projections of the light rays on to the plan, or elevation, or side elevation—and using, as necessary, verticals and lines to the vanishing points *Vr* and *Vl*—we can draw every one of the shadows.

The light point L is situated at a distance a to one side of the standpoint S and at a height h_l above it. The feet of the perpendiculars, L', L'_1, L'_2 from L in the picture plane are situated on the floor section (g), and at the heights of the chair-seat and of the table. All the light rays run parallel to $L\text{-}CV$; the shadows cast by vertical edges on to the ground are parallel to $L'\text{-}CV$, those cast on to the chair-seats are parallel to $L_1'\text{-}CV$, and so on. The point L_{wl}, the perpendicular projection of L_p on to the (extended) back wall of the room, becomes in the perspective drawing the vanishing point of all shadows cast on that wall by horizontal lines at right angles to the wall. Similarly, the point L_{wr}, the perpendicular projection of L_p on to the other side wall, becomes in the perspective drawing the vanishing point of the shadows thrown on this wall by lines perpendicular to it. The shadows are constructed using the direction of the light rays and the vanishing points; for the furniture the shadows on the ground are drawn first. The shadows on the chair-seats are obtained by going from the points where the various shadow lines cut their edges.

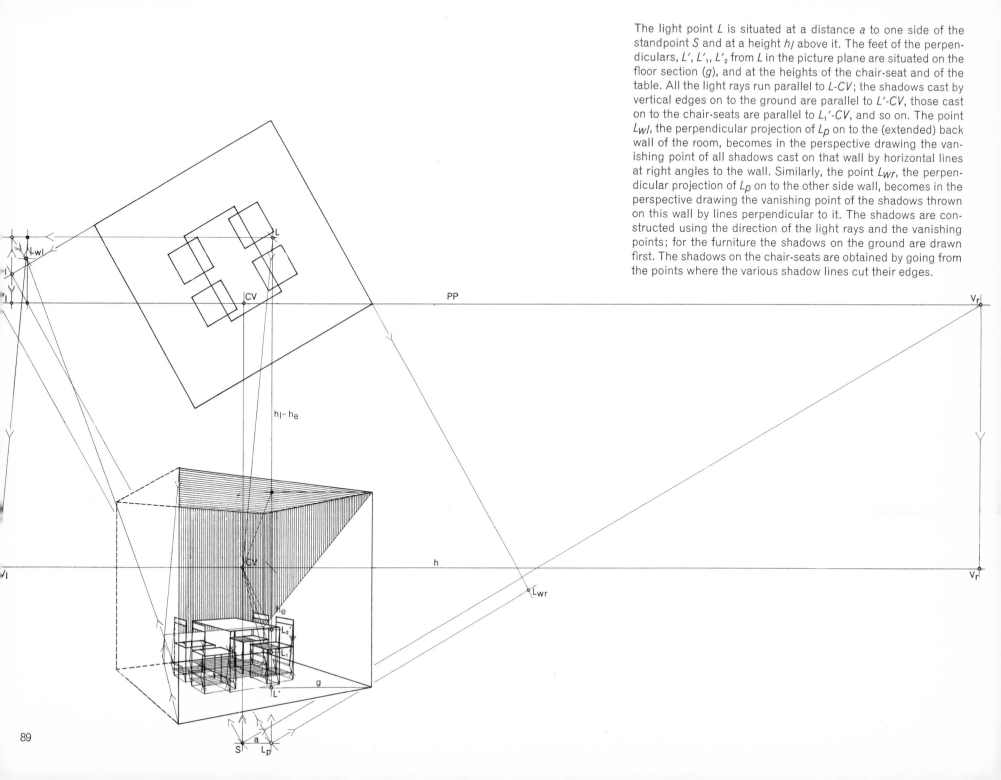

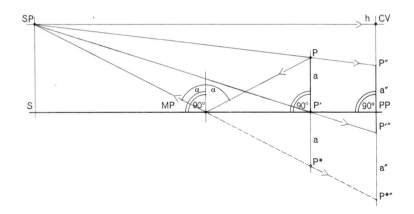

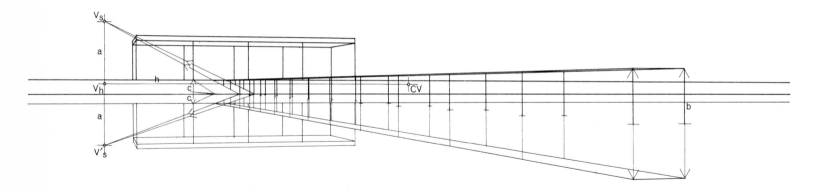

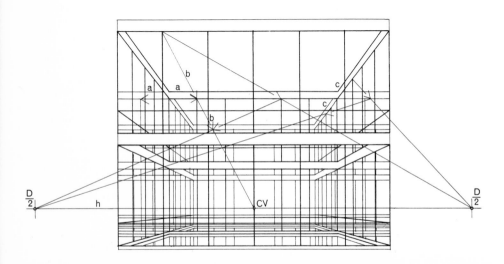

It is easy to draw reflections in perspective so long as the mirrors or reflecting surfaces are not unusually inclined or curved and do not endlessly repeat their reflections in one another.

The mirror image of any point appears to be situated as far behind the reflecting surface as the point itself is in front of it, both points lying on a line perpendicular to the plane of the reflecting surface; the surface may be supposed extended if need be.

Horizontal mirror

Reflections in water, in a polished floor, or a horizontal ceiling-mirror, and so on.

The perspective is drawn up to the reflecting surface of the water, and for each point the corresponding foot of the perpendicular from it on to the reflecting plane is determined; the reflecting plane may be continued, if need be, beyond the bank containing the water. Each perpendicular is extended below the reflecting plane so that its initial length is doubled, and this gives the image points of the reflection. The vanishing points for reflected straight lines lie on the same verticals as the vanishing points for the original lines and the horizon bisects the distance between pairs of corresponding vanishing points. The mirror images of horizontal straight lines are parallel to the original lines and both have the same vanishing points.

90

Vertical mirror parallel to the picture plane
It is particularly easy to add the reflected picture in a central perspective, if—as here—the plane of the mirror coincides with the picture plane. If the depths into the room have been constructed along the depth-line *a* by rays from the distance point D_r to a dimensioned line *b*,

then the apparent depths in the reflection can again be constructed by means of rays through the dimensioned line *b* but proceeding this time to the distance point D_l. The mirror image of a picture point in this case always lies on the same depth-line as the picture point, i. e. on the line directed towards *CV*.

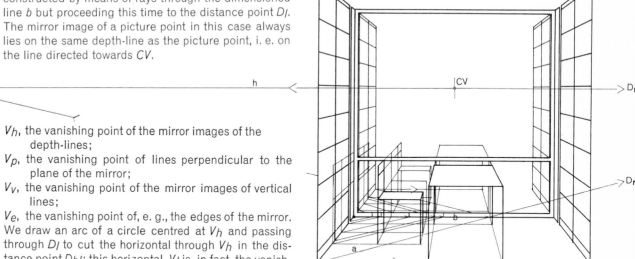

Inclined mirror intersecting the picture plane in a horizontal line a
The perspective is constructed by means of depth-lines from a cross-section of the room; the depths in the room are plotted on the line *a* starting from point *P* and are transferred on to the depth-line *dl* by vanishing lines from the distance point D_r; the depth-line, of course, runs from *P* to the centre of vision, *CV*. If the mirror is inclined at the angle α to the vertical, we construct at the distance point D_l lines inclined at the angles α and 2α to the horizontal, and also draw the lines at right angles to these. These four lines from D_l intersect the vertical line through the centre of vision in the points:

V_h, the vanishing point of the mirror images of the depth-lines;

V_p, the vanishing point of lines perpendicular to the plane of the mirror;

V_v, the vanishing point of the mirror images of vertical lines;

V_e, the vanishing point of, e. g., the edges of the mirror. We draw an arc of a circle centred at V_h and passing through D_l to cut the horizontal through V_h in the distance point D_{hl}; this horizontal V_t is, in fact, the vanishing trace of the mirror images of horizontal planes. Rays from measured points on the line *a* to D_{hl} give on the

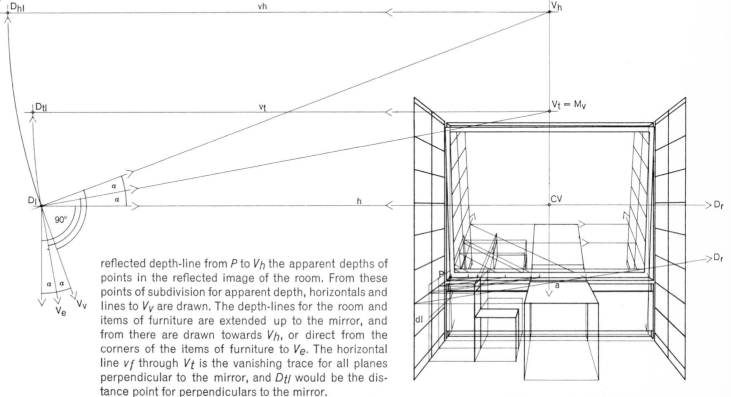

reflected depth-line from *P* to V_h the apparent depths of points in the reflected image of the room. From these points of subdivision for apparent depth, horizontals and lines to V_v are drawn. The depth-lines for the room and items of furniture are extended up to the mirror, and from there are drawn towards V_h, or direct from the corners of the items of furniture to V_e. The horizontal line *vf* through V_t is the vanishing trace for all planes perpendicular to the mirror, and D_{tl} would be the distance point for perpendiculars to the mirror.

The perspective, together with the plan (which here is on the scale 1:50), is drawn in the usual way up to the stage of putting in the reflection. The plan is then extended axially symmetrically about the mirror wall. Only that part of this extension will be visible which is included between the visual rays (drawn from *S*) through the two edge points of the mirror. The vanishing points for the extension are constructed. These vanishing points will coincide with the existing vanishing points so far as object lines go which in the plan are either parallel to or perpendicular to the mirror. But for object lines which in plan are inclined at 45° to the mirror, the vanishing points for the original lines and for their mirror images, rather surprisingly, cross over.

For object-edges which are, in reality, horizontal the perspective image lines are continued up to the mirror, and from there are extended either to the new vanishing point or to the old vanishing point as may be necessary; and so we have found the mirror images of horizontal edges. The mirror images of vertical edges are obtained by means of visual rays from *S* to the extension of the plan, verticals being drawn downwards from the points of intersection of these rays with the picture plane.

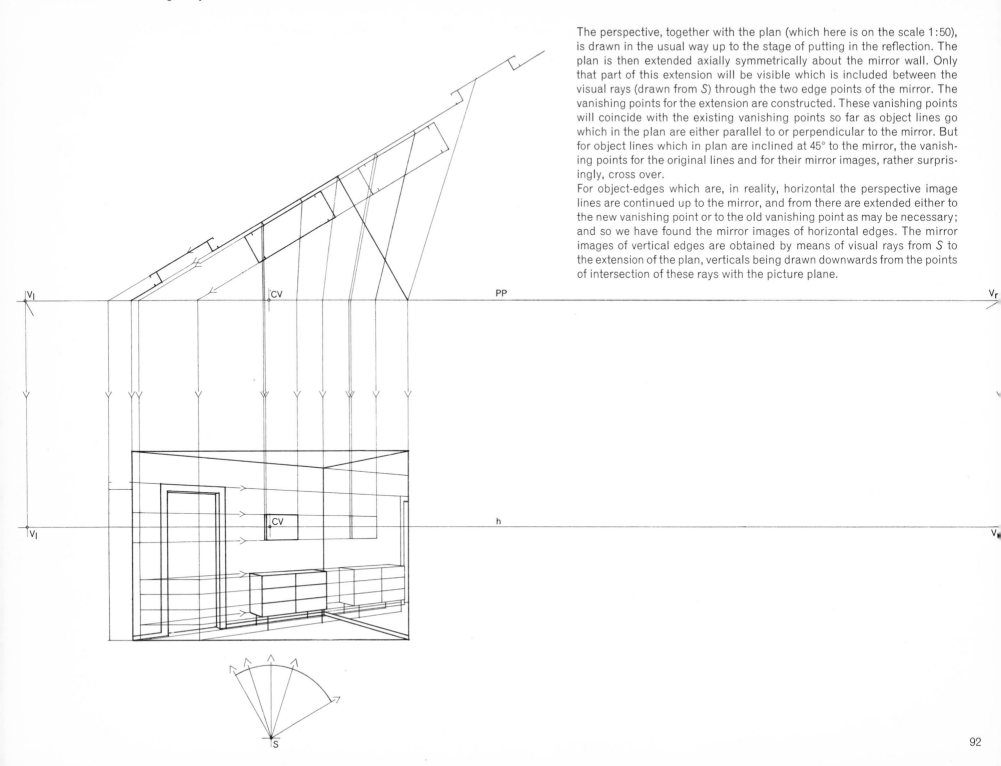

First the room is drawn in perspective by means of the plan and visual rays, a dimensioned edge in the picture plane, and the vanishing points; we continue until we reach the window in which the reflection occurs. In order to obtain the vanishing points and measuring points for the window frame and for the reflection, we first construct the measuring point M_l by means of an arc of the circle with centre V_l and passing through the standpoint S. Through M_l we draw lines inclined at the angles α and 2α to the horizon and also the two lines perpendicular to these, α being the angle of inclination of the window to the vertical; these lines fix on the vertical through V_l the points V_h, V_t, V_v, V_e.

V_h is the vanishing point of the mirror images of lines pointing towards V_l, V_v the vanishing point for the mirror images of vertical object-lines, V_t the vanishing point of lines perpendicular to the reflecting surface, and V_e the vanishing point of the side of the window.

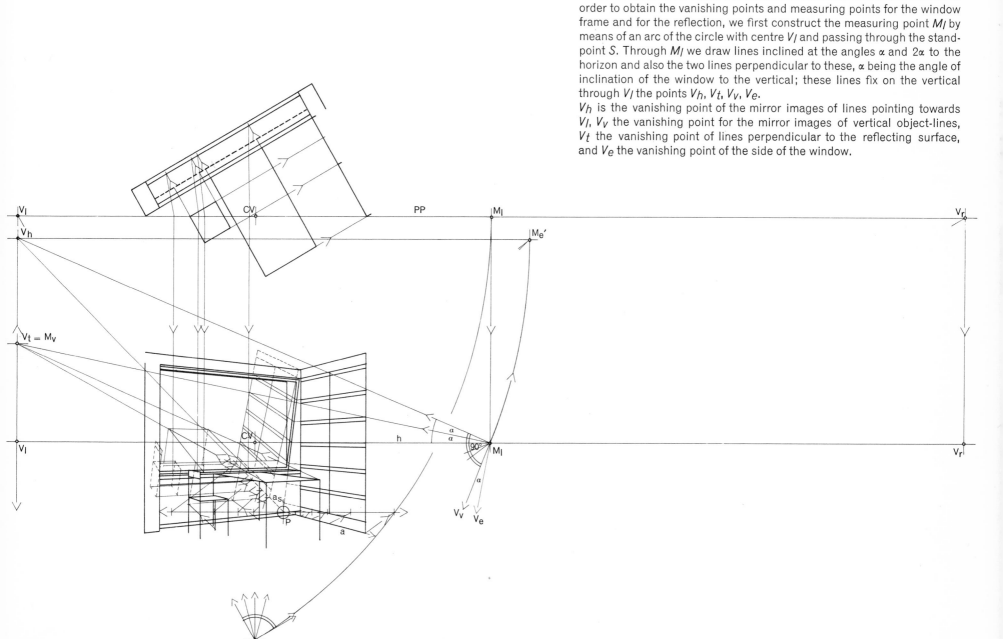

Horizontal flooring viewed axially

Decorative surfaces made up of regular triangular blocks or of squares can be drawn perspectively without using the plan. The horizon is drawn horizontally in any position, and at a distance equal to the height of eye, h_e, below it we put in the ground line or floor trace, g (the intersection of the floor with the picture plane). The subdivisions for the blocks are marked off along g on the same scale as was used for h_e. The centre of vision, CV, is marked on the horizon centrally above these subdivisions. To the right or left of CV on h, or on both sides at equal — not too short — distance. We mark off the diagonal or 60° vanishing points and stick pins them and CV. The vanishing lines are drawn in lightly with a hard, sharp-pointed pencil. One part of the flooring is now almost done. Horizontals are drawn through the points of intersection. The vanishing lines, which are still missing, can be drawn through the points of intersection of the horizontals, with the other vanishing lines.

For more complicated kinds of flooring or in more complicated perspectives, we have to construct vanishing points and measuring points in the plan, as shown in the examples.

To make a perspective drawing of a pattern on a horizontal ceiling, the construction is similar to that just described, but is inverted. We start from a ceiling line drawn at a height above the horizon equal to the difference between the room height and the height of eye. To represent the pattern on a side wall perpendicular to the picture plane, a similar construction at the side is used.

To draw a perspective of patterns on floors and ceilings which run horizontally along depth-lines but slope transversely, we start from a dimensioned cross-section of the room and a given horizon and centre of vision. The vanishing point for the inclined floor lines, however, does not lie on the given horizon but on a sloping line through the centre of vision parallel to the floor or ceiling section. Since the length of the sloping side is greater than its plan projection, the question now arises whether the pattern has been constructed by subdividing the sloping length into a number of equal parts and using blocks which are actually rectangles instead of squares, for instance, or whether the pattern really does consist of given, uniform blocks.

In the first case, the distance of the vanishing point from the centre of vision is constructed by first thinking of the pattern as drawn in the horizontal ground plane, determining the vanishing point and erecting a vertical there to intersect the vanishing trace of the inclined plane. In the second case, the vanishing point determined for the pattern in the horizontal plane is brought up to the van-

ishing trace by means of a circular arc with centre at the centre of vision.

Sloping flooring, viewed frontally

A flooring which is horizontal in the transverse direction but which slopes upward or downward in the direction looking into the picture will have a horizontal vanishing trace h', situated at a distance above or below the horizon equal to the distance d multiplied by the slope. This vanishing trace can be constructed in two ways: either we plot the angle of slope, α, at the diagonal point D (situated at the distance d from CV) and so obtain the point CV' on the vanishing trace vertically above CV, or as in bottom left diagram, p. 97, we draw a line at S inclined at the angle α to the principal visual ray and so obtain the height a of the vanishing trace as the distance along the picture plane of the point of intersection from CV.

The construction of the vanishing points and measuring points proceeds differently, because the vanishing points are determined by specifying angles whereas the measuring points depend on the position of the vanishing points and their distance from the station point. To obtain the vanishing points for the sloping pattern, we draw the vanishing points for the pattern thought of as lying in the horizontal plane, and the corresponding measuring points. If the plane of the pattern is now inclined upwards at the angle α to the horizontal, the parallels to the pattern lines drawn through the station point will correspondingly be inclined upwards. As this happens, the vanishing points will move outwards from one another along hyperbolic tracks (see page 95, lower left). The centre of vision (which in the side-elevation represents the whole horizon) is related, centre S, until it meets the line drawn at S with the inclination α. Through the point so found a line is drawn parallel to the picture plane. On pages 95 and 96, lower left, it has been found somewhat differently. All the vanishing points are transferred on to it perpendicularly, again projected on to the picture plane, and from this are drawn perpendicularly to the vanishing trace of the sloping flooring at a distance equal to a above the horizon. To obtain the measuring points, for example the diagonal point D', we construct first the measuring points, situated on the horizon h, for the pattern supposed horizontal. The measuring points for the sloping pattern are then obtained by means of circular arcs drawn with centre at the new centre of vision CV' to cut the horizontal vanishing trace h' for the sloping pattern. Once the vanishing and measuring points have been determined, and the starting points have been measured off along the ground line g, the construction proceeds as for the horizontal flooring.

Horizontal flooring viewed diagonally

We consider first how to obtain the undistorted pattern most easily. The vanishing points V, etc., for the directions found will be obtained by lines through the standpoint parallel to these directions cutting the picture plane trace PP; if the picture plane and the horizon are not the same, then perpendiculars will be erected upwards at these points. If all the vanishing points are accessible there is no difficulty. The outline of the surface and its subdivisions are obtained as usual by means of vanishing lines, visual rays and perpendiculars, or, as shown in the example, by means of scales along the ground line g starting from the point P in the picture plane, and by vanishing lines and rays from the measuring points. Inaccessible vanishing points must be replaced by using the radial arms device or by perspective subdivision of a transverse vanishing line. The measuring point for an inaccessible vanishing point is obtained by constructing at the standpoint against the principal visual ray half the angle β between picture plane and flooring line.

Sloping patterned surface viewed diagonally

Here again we first find the vanishing points for the pattern as if it were horizontal. If the surface is then tilted upward through the angle α about the edge parallel to the vanishing direction $S\text{-}V_r$, the vanishing trace of this plane will be rotated upward about the point V_r in the figure. The direction of the new vanishing trace h' is determined by finding VL', the point of intersection of the vertical through V_l with the upper arm of an angle α constructed at the measuring point M_l. All the vanishing points on the horizon, as a result of this tilting, rotate on a cone with axis $S\text{-}V_r$ in circles of various sizes which, in plan, appear as straight lines parallel to $S\text{-}V_l$. If we rotate V_l about M_l on to the line $V_l\text{-}M_l$, bring the point so obtained vertically down on to the picture plane, rotate this point about V_l on to the line $V_l\text{-}S$, we get the point $VL°$, which shows how far V_l has moved from the picture plane due to the rotation. The plan position of the rotated horizon goes through the point $VL°$ and V_r. The process again becomes different for vanishing points and measuring points. All the vanishing points, e. g., D_r, V_l, V_k, are transferred parallel to $V_l\text{-}S$ on to the rotated horizon, are then projected back on to the picture plane from the standpoint S, and finally are moved up vertically on to the vanishing trace $VL'\text{-}V_r$.

The measuring points ML', ML'', etc., are obtained simply by rotating the measuring points already found for the horizontal pattern round the new vanishing points on to the new vanishing trace. After the measuring points and vanishing points have been determined, the drawing of

Square Pattern, Horizontal

For explanation, see opposite page

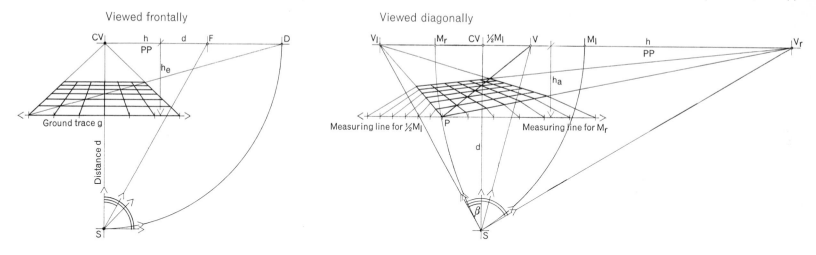

Viewed frontally

Viewed diagonally

Sloping Square Pattern

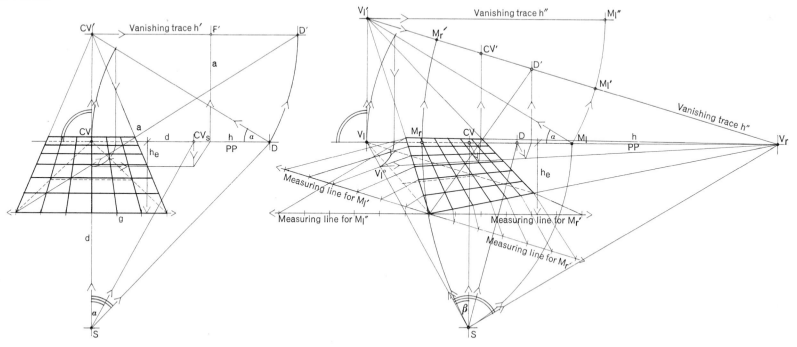

the flooring proceeds in the same way as for a horizontal, patterned floor. The measuring lines are always parallel to the vanishing traces, i. e. the straight lines through the vanishing point and the corresponding measuring

point. The subdivisions are always plotted from a point of intersection with the picture plane. If there is not enough room for a measuring line the scale may be reduced in any ratio 1/n provided that the distance of the

measuring point from the vanishing point is reduced in the same ratio 1/n.

See pages 95–97 for examples.

Horizontal Hexagonal Pattern

Viewed frontally

Viewed diagonally

Sloping Hexagonal Pattern

Viewed frontally

Viewed diagonally

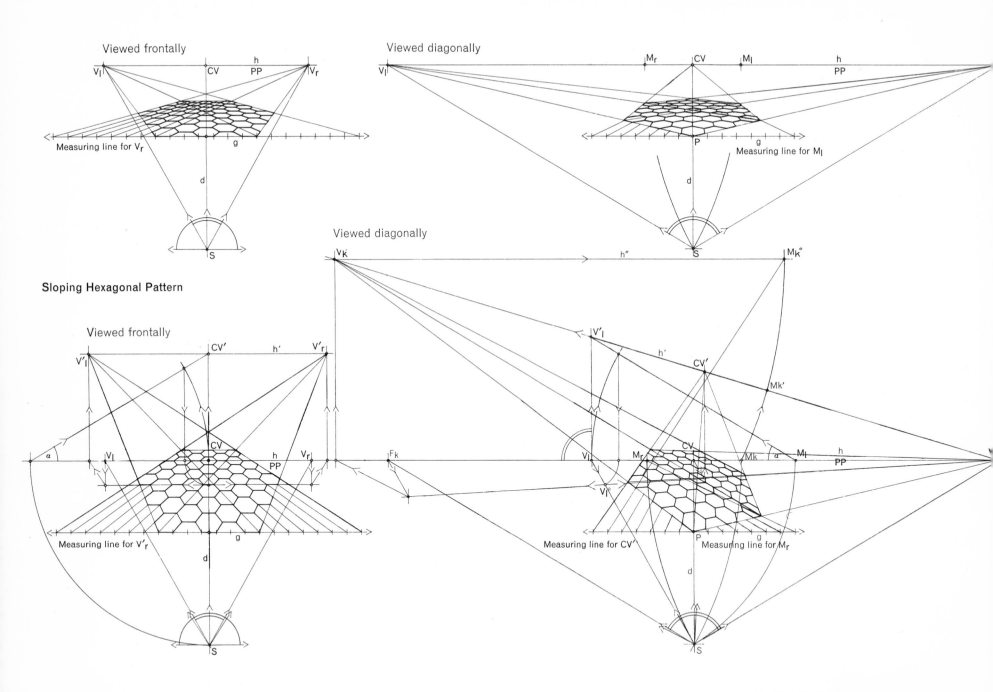

For explanation, see page 94

Horizontal Octagonal Pattern

Viewed frontally

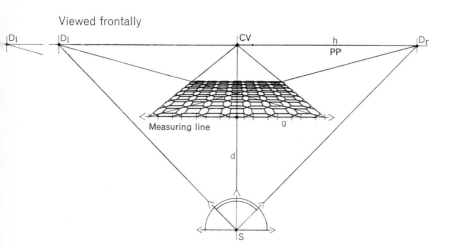

Viewed diagonally

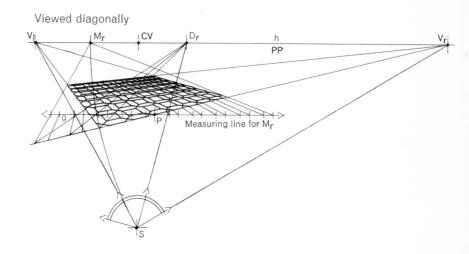

Sloping Octagonal Pattern

Viewed frontally

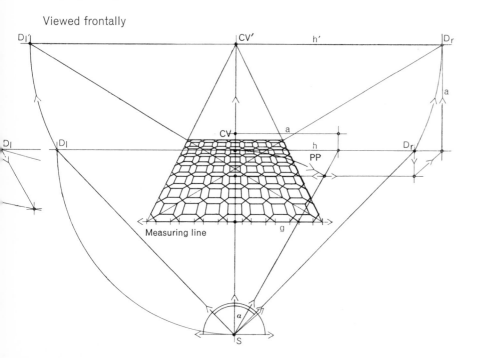

Viewed diagonally

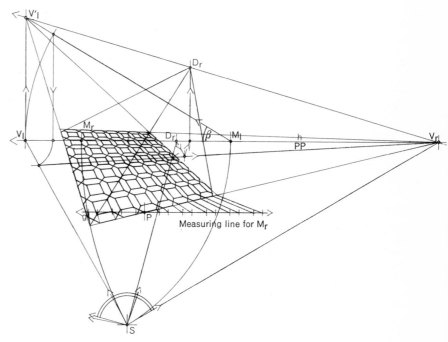

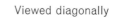

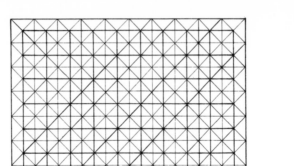

The framework consists of simple members fastened together to form halves of octahedra. The angles α and β are the inclinations to the horizontal of the sloping edges and faces respectively of the octahedra, and these are determined as shown in the adjoining diagram. The horizontal elements of the framework form a regular square pattern and are drawn in central perspective as already described for a squared flooring; that is, by means of depth-lines and a diagonal. The vanishing traces for the transverse octahedral surfaces are obtained by drawing lines through CV inclined to the horizontal at the angle β, the inclination of these octahedral surfaces. Where these vanishing traces cut the verticals through the diagonal points D_l and D_r we have the vanishing points V_{lu} and V_{ru} (V_{ll} and V_{rl}) for the rising (falling) directions along the sloping elements of the framework. These points could also be obtained as the intersections with the verticals through D_l and D_r of lines drawn through the measuring points M_{dr} and M_{dl} at inclination α to the horizontal. The upper horizontal stiffeners of the framework are again drawn in the same way as a squared horizontal surface is drawn in central perspective.

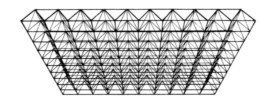

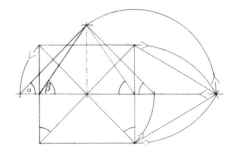

Perspective of a Space Frame in the Form of a Pentagonal Pavilion Roof

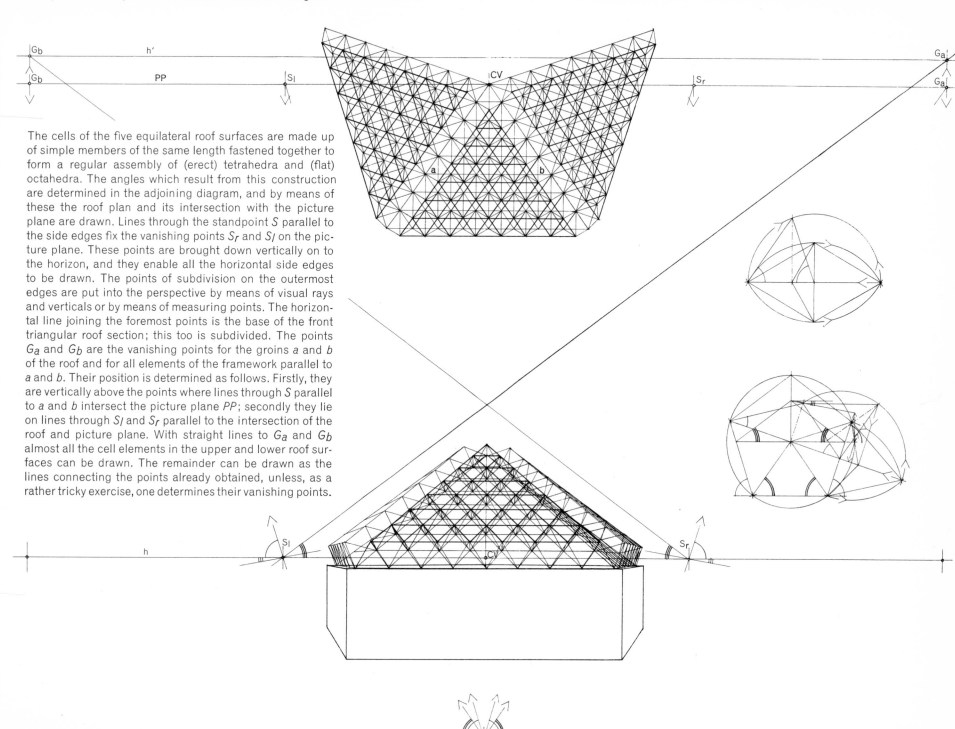

The cells of the five equilateral roof surfaces are made up of simple members of the same length fastened together to form a regular assembly of (erect) tetrahedra and (flat) octahedra. The angles which result from this construction are determined in the adjoining diagram, and by means of these the roof plan and its intersection with the picture plane are drawn. Lines through the standpoint S parallel to the side edges fix the vanishing points S_r and S_l on the picture plane. These points are brought down vertically on to the horizon, and they enable all the horizontal side edges to be drawn. The points of subdivision on the outermost edges are put into the perspective by means of visual rays and verticals or by means of measuring points. The horizontal line joining the foremost points is the base of the front triangular roof section; this too is subdivided. The points G_a and G_b are the vanishing points for the groins a and b of the roof and for all elements of the framework parallel to a and b. Their position is determined as follows. Firstly, they are vertically above the points where lines through S parallel to a and b intersect the picture plane PP; secondly they lie on lines through S_l and S_r parallel to the intersection of the roof and picture plane. With straight lines to G_a and G_b almost all the cell elements in the upper and lower roof surfaces can be drawn. The remainder can be drawn as the lines connecting the points already obtained, unless, as a rather tricky exercise, one determines their vanishing points.

General remarks
The vanishing point for lines parallel to the slope of the stairs lies on the vertical through the vanishing point to which the horizontal edges of the steps or the horizontal edges of the side walls point. At the measuring point corresponding to the distance of the latter vanishing point from the standpoint a line is drawn inclined to the horizontal at the angle of slope of the steps. Where this cuts the vertical line is the vanishing point for lines parallel to the slope.

Plan and section, scale 1:50. Width of steps 5 m. (16 ft. 6 in.), 35 steps 15/30 cm. (6/12 in.).

In the plan a standpoint is chosen in front of the steps corresponding to an angle of vision of between 30° and 40°. The picture plane is drawn, if possible, through the front edge of one of the steps. This front edge is drawn directly below the plan and at a height h_e below the arbitrarily chosen horizon h. The perspective images of the horizontal side edges of the steps converge towards the centre of vision CV. The perspective lines for the slope of the steps must converge towards a point V_S situated vertically above CV. The height h_S of this point can be obtained by drawing a line through S inclined to the principal visual rays at an angle corresponding to the slope (here 15/30 = 1:2). This slope line cuts the picture plane in P and the distance from CV to P is equal to the required height h_S. Two methods are available for drawing the side edges of the steps between the vanishing lines for the steps; either we project from S the plan positions on to the picture plane and then drop perpendiculars to intersect the vanishing lines, as shown at the left of the diagram; or we can mark off equal divisions along the extended vertical edge of the front step and use the depth-lines from the points of subdivision to the centre of vision, as shown at the right of the diagram. The handrails as a rule will be about 90 cm. (3 ft..) above and 5 to 10 cm. (2 to 4 in.) inward from the front edge of the first step at the point where they intersect the picture plane. They converge towards the vanishing point V_S. The ends and corners in the handrail can be constructed by means of vertical lines through the front edges of the steps or treads.

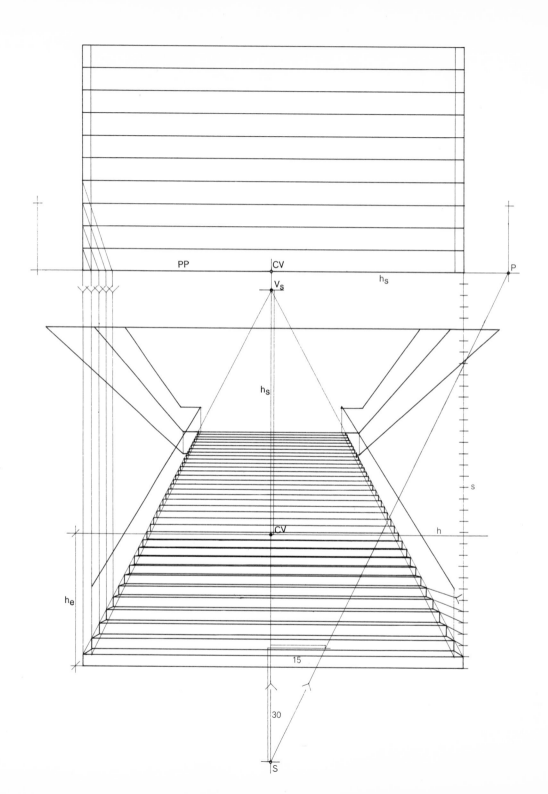

100

Plan scale 1 : 50. Widths of steps 6.50 m. (21 ft. 4 in.),
2×16 steps 15/30 cm (6/12 in.)
If a staircase is to be drawn as if viewed almost frontally
but yet not exactly along its axis, difficulties arise because one vanishing point will be inaccessible. It is
then best to arrange the staircase plan so that the vertical edge of one step is in the picture plane. The standpoint S is positioned to give a suitable angle of vision,
and through S a line is drawn parallel to the axis of the
staircase to intersect the picture plane in the point V.
Here a line is drawn at right angles to S-V, and at S
another line is drawn to form with S-V an angle equal to
the slope of the staircase (here 15/30 = 1:2). These two
lines intersect in the point A, and the distance V-A is
equal to the distance h_S of the vanishing points V_u and
V_l from V, the vanishing point for the side edges of the
steps. V_u is the vanishing point for lines running upward
parallel to the slope of the steps and is above V, while V_l
is the vanishing point for the lines running downward (in
the second flight of steps) parallel to the slope and is
below V. The horizon h is drawn below the plan in a position such that both these vanishing points V_u and V_l
at the distances h_S above and below h will fall on the
drawing-board. The vanishing points are located on the
vertical dropped from V in the plan.
The two vertical transverse planes which limit the width
of the staircase intersect the picture plane in the points
B and C, and from these points the verticals s are brought
down into the perspective. On these lines s all the heights
can be plotted (on the scale 1:50); first the height of eye
h_e (here 1.80 m. [6 ft.]) is plotted to give the ground
line and then the scale for the step heights, starting
from the bottom upwards. The horizontal side edges
of the steps all lie on the lines drawn from these scales
to the vanishing point V on the horizon. On the side (C)
where the steps start in the picture plane, using the pair
of vanishing lines to V_u and V_l, we can soon complete the
construction. On the opposite side, we argue that, if the
steps were continued forward into the picture plane, they
would fall (or rise) by a further amount $a \times 15/30 = a/2$,
where a is the distance BB' in the plan. So we draw the
vanishing lines through initial points which are plotted
at a distance $a/2$ lower and higher respectively, and then
the construction at this side can also be completed. The
joining lines of two consecutive points of intersection
represent the vertical edges of the steps and the points
should be vertically one above the other if the drawing
is accurate. Having fixed the right and left end points,
their joins represent the nearer and further horizontal
edges of the steps.

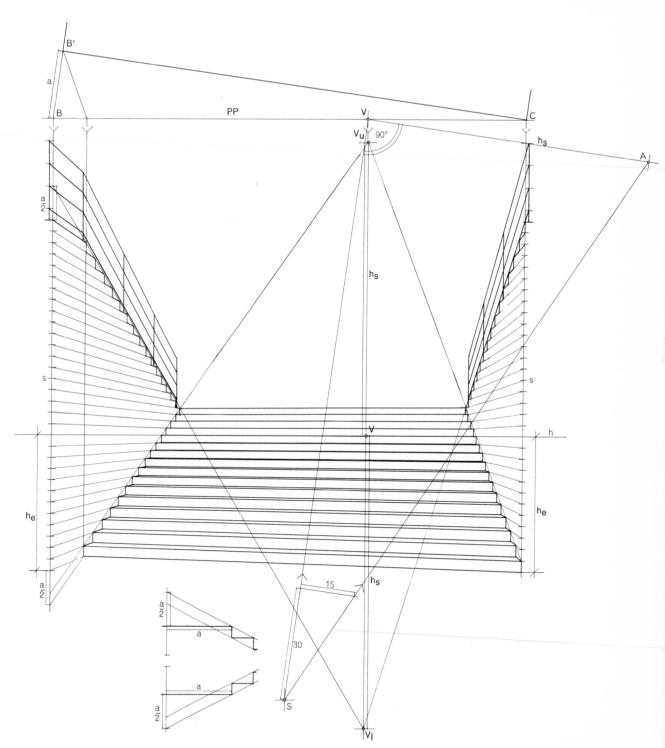

Diagonal Perspective of a Cantilevered Stairway

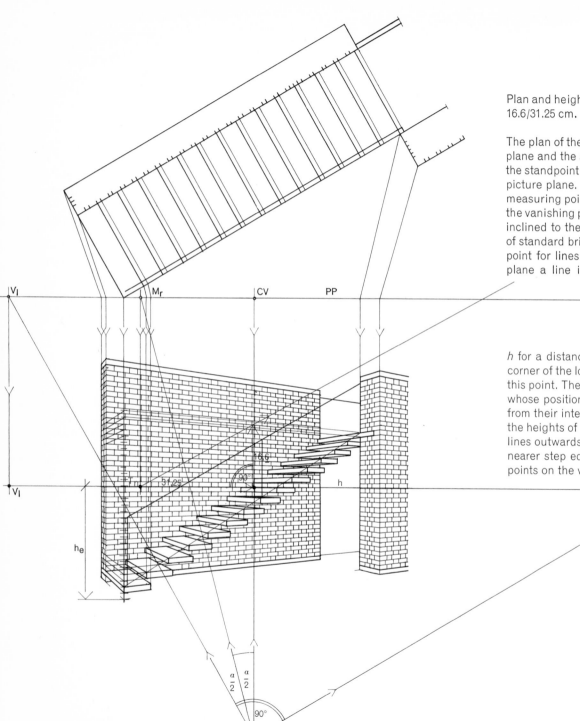

Plan and heights in the picture plane to scale 1:50; width of steps 1.25 m. (4 ft.), 15 steps 16.6/31.25 cm. ($6^1/_2$/12 in.).

The plan of the staircase is arranged with the corner of the bottom step in the picture plane and the standpoint is chosen at a suitable distance in front of it. Lines through the standpoint parallel to the edges of the steps determine the vanishing points on the picture plane. A visual ray inclined at $\alpha/2$ to the principal visual ray determines the measuring point M_r. The horizon h is drawn in, parallel to the picture plane trace, and the vanishing points and measuring point are marked on it. At M_r (on h) a line is drawn inclined to the horizon at the angle of slope 16.6/31.25 (which arises from the shape of standard bricks) and is produced to cut the vertical through V_r in V_s, the vanishing point for lines parallel to the slope of the stairs. From the step corner in the picture plane a line is drawn vertically downwards and is continued below the horizon

h for a distance equal to the height of eye. This defines the position of the bottom corner of the lowest step, and the heights of the bricks are marked off vertically above this point. The vanishing lines to V_l determine the heights on the side face of the wall whose position sideways is fixed by rays from S to the plan and verticals downward from their intersections with the picture plane. Then vanishing lines to V_r determine the heights of all the rows of bricks and of the steps on the wall face, while vanishing lines outwards from the measured edge in the picture plane give the heights for the nearer step edges. The hand-rail points to V_s, and the lines through corresponding points on the various steps must also converge to V_s (this serves as a check).

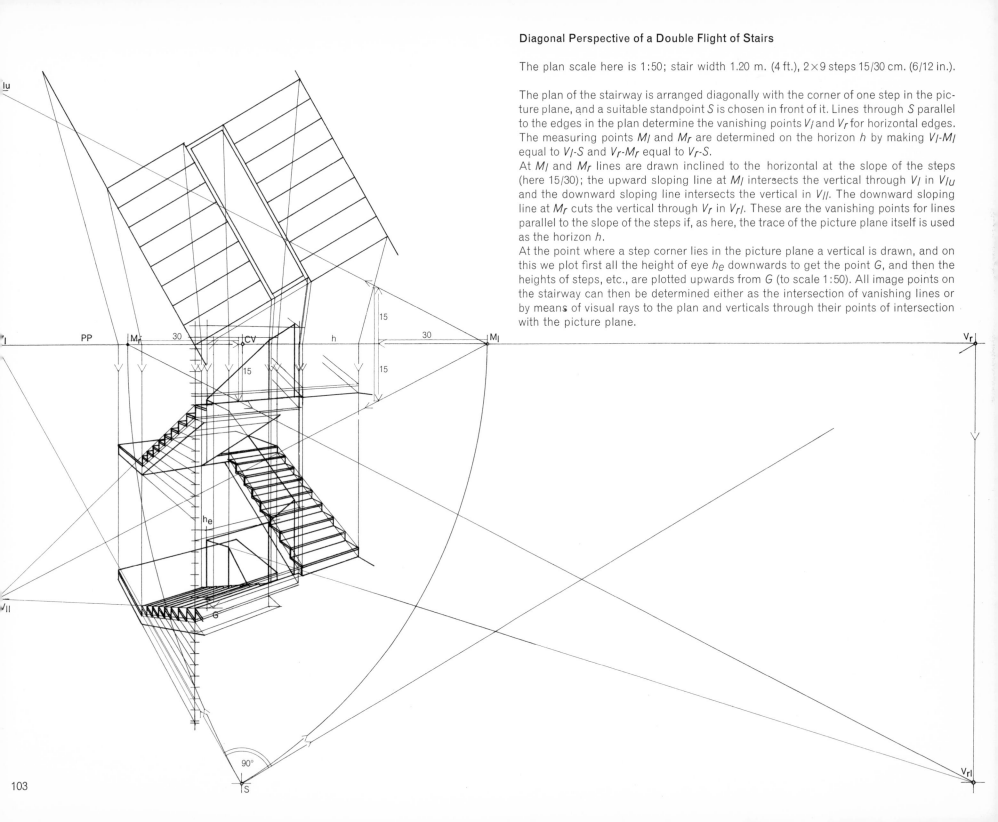

Diagonal Perspective of a Double Flight of Stairs

The plan scale here is 1:50; stair width 1.20 m. (4 ft.), 2×9 steps 15/30 cm. (6/12 in.).

The plan of the stairway is arranged diagonally with the corner of one step in the picture plane, and a suitable standpoint S is chosen in front of it. Lines through S parallel to the edges in the plan determine the vanishing points V_l and V_r for horizontal edges. The measuring points M_l and M_r are determined on the horizon h by making V_l-M_l equal to V_l-S and V_r-M_r equal to V_r-S.

At M_l and M_r lines are drawn inclined to the horizontal at the slope of the steps (here 15/30); the upward sloping line at M_l intersects the vertical through V_l in V_{lu} and the downward sloping line intersects the vertical in V_{ll}. The downward sloping line at M_r cuts the vertical through V_r in V_{rl}. These are the vanishing points for lines parallel to the slope of the steps if, as here, the trace of the picture plane itself is used as the horizon h.

At the point where a step corner lies in the picture plane a vertical is drawn, and on this we plot first all the height of eye h_e downwards to get the point G, and then the heights of steps, etc., are plotted upwards from G (to scale 1:50). All image points on the stairway can then be determined either as the intersection of vanishing lines or by means of visual rays to the plan and verticals through their points of intersection with the picture plane.

Spiral Staircase

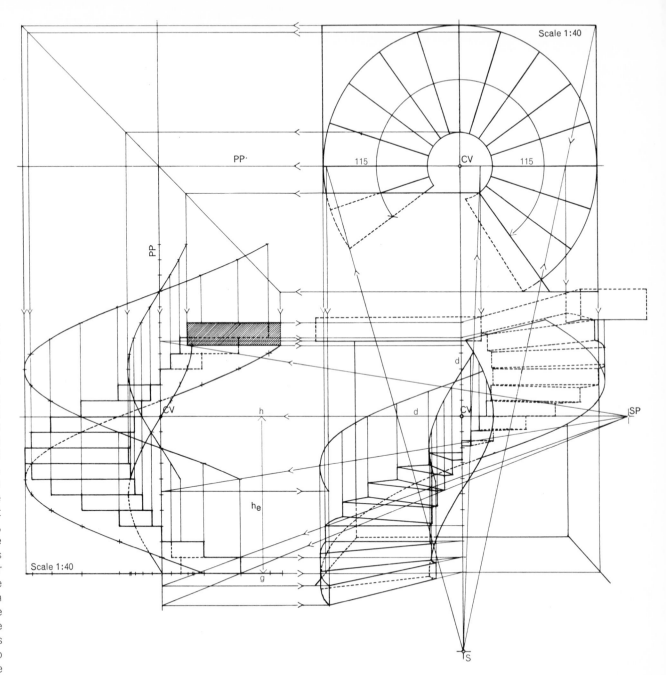

Plan and elevation to scale 1:40. Width of step 1.15 m. (3 ft. 9 in.), diameter of eye 0.70 m. (28 in.), handrail height 0.83 m. (33 in.), 16 steps 16.6/30 cm. (7/12 in.).

The picture plane goes through the axis of the staircase and the standpoint is placed so far in front of it that the visual angle does not exceed 40°. The points of intersection with the picture plane of visual rays from S to object points in the plan, when brought down vertically into the perspective, determine the positions in the left-to-right direction of the corresponding image points.

An exact side elevation of the staircase—which may, if necessary, be built up from a 45° reflection of the plan and the specified heights—is placed to the side of, and at an arbitrary distance below, the trace of the picture plane. In the elevation the picture plane again intersects the axis of the staircase and it will appear as a vertical line. The station point SP at eye-level ($h_e = 1.60$ m. [5 ft. 3 in.]) has the same distance as in the plan: $d = CV\text{-}SP = CV\text{-}S$. The points of intersection with the (vertical) picture plane of visual rays from SP to object points in the elevation, when brought across horizontally, give the height of the corresponding image points in the perspective. It is advisable to number the object points in the plan and in the elevation to ensure that the proper horizontal and vertical are used to determine each image point and so to avoid the errors which otherwise can easily be made. The work of drawing in the perspective the heights of the steps and the handrail at the eye of the staircase can be avoided by first determining the heights at the outer string and then remembering that the step edges and the joins of points of equal heights on the handrails point to the scale on the stair axis (drawn here to scale 1:40), because this axis lies in the picture plane. Horizontal straight lines in the under surface of the staircase boards, if there are any, cannot point towards the axis of the staircase.

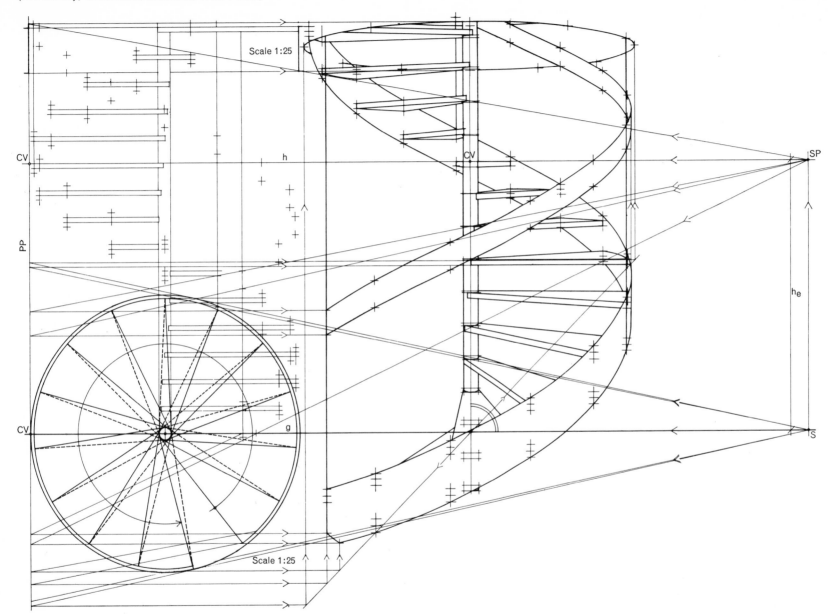

Spiral Staircase
(Art Gallery, Darmstadt; architect, Theo Pabst)

Scale 1:25

Scale 1:25

Storey height 2.70 m. (8 ft. 10 in.), diameter 1.90 m. (6 ft. 5 in.), 15 steps 18/26 cm. (7/10 in.).

The plan and elevation of the staircase are drawn, on the scale 1:25, one directly below the other at the left-hand side of the drawing area. For simplicity the inner part of the handrail has been omitted. The picture plane is taken right on the outside, touching the aperture through the

ceiling; the station point *SP* is arranged at a suitable distance and at the height of eye, 1.80 m. (6 ft.), on the other side of the elevation. Visual rays from *SP* to object points in the elevation determine on the picture plane the heights of the corresponding image points. The standpoint *S* lies vertically below the station point on the horizontal through the staircase axis in the plan. Visual rays from *S* to the object in plan determine on the pic-

ture plane the width of the image. Heights of image points are taken across horizontally; the widths may be transferred using either a paper strip or dividers, or, as shown in the diagram, by horizontal rays reflected into the vertical by a reflecting line inclined at 45° to the horizontal. The perspective picture results from joining the points constructed in this way.

Staircase between Four Floors Viewed Transversely, Drawn using Auxiliary Perspective Sketches

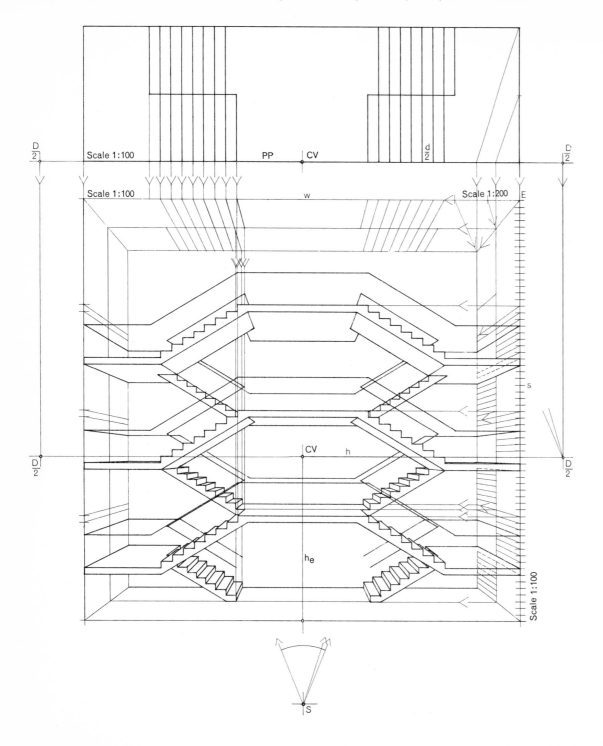

Storey height 2.80 m. (9 ft.), step width 1.80 m. (6 ft.),
6×8 steps 17.5/30 cm. (7/12 in.).

The plan (to scale 1:100) is arranged with the front edges
of the steps in the picture plane, and so the whole of the
nearer stringers appears in the perspective as a 1:100
elevation. To minimize the distortion the height of eye
has been taken as 4.40 m. (14 ft. 6 in.). The standpoint
is placed at a sufficiently large distance d in front of the
picture plane; the centre of vision and the half-distance
point are determined and brought down on to the horizon.
Depth-lines from the front surface of the staircase to the
centre of vision give the perspective images of the edges
of the steps. Above the picture, starting from a measuring line w, we draw a perspective plan by means of
depth-lines; and at the side, starting from a measuring
line s, we similarly draw a perspective elevation. Depths
into the picture can be determined by either (A) the intersections with the depth-line through the point E of
the rays from the half-distance point $D/2$ to a measuring
line for depths on the scale $\frac{1}{2}$:100 $= 1$:200 through E;
or (B) visual rays from S and verticals through their points
of intersection with the picture plane.
Widths in the perspective are transferred down vertically
from the perspective plan, and heights in the perspective
are transferred horizontally from the perspective elevation. All lines parallel to the picture plane will, of course,
appear with their true inclination and shapes.

In perspective representations of circles all the conic sections may appear. If the plane of an object-circle intersects the station point, the circle will appear as a straight line. If a circle is parallel to the picture plane its perspective image is a circle again. The images of other circles behind the picture plane are always ellipses, though it can sometimes happen that the ellipse has principal axes of equal length and thus appears as a circle. Circles which touch a plane through the station point parallel to the picture plane—the so-called vanishing plane—will appear as parabolas; if they intersect the vanishing plane, they appear as hyperbolas. It is rare for circles to appear as parabolas or hyperbolas, so this case is not discussed here.

When we want to draw a curve such as a circle in perspective, we pick out the important points or those most easily constructed, and similarly tangents, axes, and diameters, and draw this net of lines in perspective. To draw a small circle in perspective it suffices to draw the perspective of a single square surrounding it; for a somewhat larger circle, the block of four squares formed by a square touching the circle and the diameters joining the points of contact; for a larger circle still, the block of four squares just described together with the two diagonals; and for the largest circles, we draw the perspective of the eight-pointed star formed by two blocks of four squares, one rotated through 45° relative to the other (see the upper diagram). In the first case, the perspective outline is just a trapezium, in which we have to draw an ellipse touching the sides at about their midpoints; in the second case, the four points of contact are accurately determined; in the last case we have four more points fixed for the image of the circle and also the direction of the curve at these points.

Determination of the axes of the elliptical image
If the polar axis of an object-circle, i. e. its axis of rotation, intersects the principal visual ray—if, for example, the circle lies horizontally directly in front of the standpoint—then the perspective image of the circumscribing square (formed from depth-lines and parallels to the picture plane) will be a symmetrical trapezium, and it will be particularly easy to determine the *axes* of the image ellipse. The first axis lies on the depth line forming the line of symmetry. The other axis is along the perpendicular line through the centre, since an ellipse is always symmetrical about *two* perpendicular diameters. The visual rays which produce the end-points of the diameter the ellipse are, in the plan, tangents to the circle. Their points of contact do *not* lie on the circumscribing square: the image of the centre of the circle is not the

centre of the image ellipse. With the axes known, it is easy to draw even large ellipses using the thread method described on page 16 (top right).
If the trapezium-shaped, perspectively deformed circumscribing quadrilateral should be asymmetric, then it would be harder to determine the principal axes of the ellipse. It would then be better to start in another way, circumscribing the circle by a trapezium which in perspective would become a parallelogram; but the construction is really only practicable for particular horizontal circles.

Representation of a circle using a circumscribing trapezium
(see the lower diagram)
A depth-line is drawn through the centre of the circle to be represented; in plan, this cuts the vanishing plane *VP* in a point *V* to one side of the standpoint *S*, and tangents are drawn from *V* to the circle. The points where the lines cross the picture plane are plotted in the perspective at the height of the circle in elevation (h_e, h_z). Through the centre point a straight line is drawn to the centre of vision *CV* and parallels are drawn through the other points. The circle in plan is completely enclosed by a further two lines parallel to the picture plane. The perspective image of this circumscribing trapezium is the required parallelogram circumscribing the image ellipse. Its second conjugate axis can be drawn parallel to the picture plane through the point of intersection of the diagonals of this parallelogram. The conjugate axes being drawn, the true rectangular axes can be constructed using Rytz's construction (see page 18, bottom right).

A sphere will appear in perspective as a circle only if its centre lies on the principal visual ray from the station point to the centre of vision, and if all the sphere is in front of the station point. If the sphere is situated in front of the station point but not centrally in the picture, then it will appear as an ellipse. If the sphere touches the vanishing plane, i.e. the plane through the station point parallel to the picture plane, then its perspective image is a parabola; and if the sphere intersects the vanishing plane, then it appears in the perspective as a hyperbola. Only the first two of these cases are discussed here, since they occur by far the most frequently. In drawing a sphere in perspective the two most important points of the sphere are those which are closest to and furthest from the picture plane; they become the foci of the image curve in the perspective. Spheres which are situated obliquely in front of the station point at the edge of a picture with a large angle of vision appear unrealistically distorted, being elongated in the direction away from

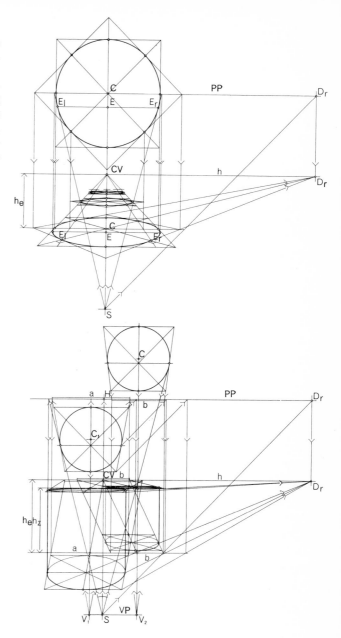

the centre of vision. This is one of the most striking instances where a perspective drawing does not correspond to actual appearance.

Horizontal Circles

To draw a perspective of a cylinder with several horizontal divisions, such as a pillar or an advertising column, the picture plane is taken to be in contact with the nearest generator of the cylinder. The standpoint S is chosen at a suitable position in front of it, and the distance points D_l, D_r on the picture plane PP are determined by lines drawn from S at 45° to that plane. The picture comes between the object plan and the station point; first the horizon h with the centre of vision CV and the distance points D_l and D_r marked off on it, and then the horizontal straight lines in which the circle planes cut the picture plane. Depth-lines and diagonals in the plan are drawn up to the picture plane, and the points of intersection are brought down vertically into the perspective. From the points of subdivision so obtained on the horizontal lines, depth-lines are drawn to the centre of vision and diagonals to the distance points. Horizontal lines through points of intersection of the depth-lines and diagonals complete the perspective representation of the squares circumscribing the circles. The tangents at the points of the circumference cut by a diagonal diameter are themselves diagonal lines, because a tangent to a circle is perpendicular to the diameter through its point of contact. These provide a useful aid in drawing the image ellipses. The furthest sideways points on the ellipses, i. e. points corresponding to the transverse boundaries of the cylinder, can be obtained by means of visual rays tangent to the plan circle, the points of intersection with the picture plane being brought down vertically into the perspective. In the perspective they lie on the line midway between the two parallels which form the nearer and farther sides of the perspective squares.

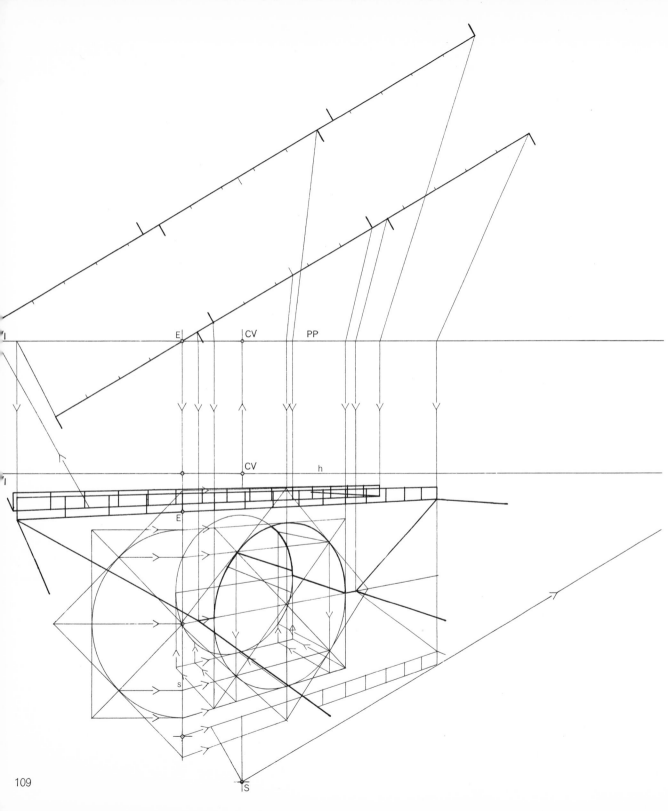

Vertical Circles

The plan here is drawn on the scale 1:200 and the drawing is arranged as usual. A circle on the object is in a vertical plane which intersects the picture plane in the vertical line *s*.

1. If this intersection *s* is situated in the drawing area, we shift the circle in its own plane until its centre lies on the picture plane. Knowing the given height of the circle, we can draw a semicircle, with the necessary points and auxiliary lines, on the same scale as in the plan.

The heights of the various points on the circle are transferred across horizontally on to *s*, the line of intersection of the picture plane and the circle plane. The horizontal distances of circle points from the centre of the circle are marked on the plan of the object, and are projected on to the picture plane by visual rays from *S*; verticals are drawn through the points of intersection with the picture plane. The points of intersection of these verticals with the vanishing lines gives the image points of the 8-pointed star circumscribing the object circle. The joining lines between some of these image points have still to be drawn in.

2. If the circle plane intersects the picture plane in an inaccessible region, and if perhaps the vanishing point for horizontals in the circle plane is also inaccessible, we can still draw the semicircle (to plan size) at the right height and in an arbitrary sideways position in the picture. We can adopt points and auxiliary lines from it, draw horizontals through these points and plot in the horizontal distances of circle points from the vertical axis of the circle in the plan. Visual rays are drawn to circle points in the plan, and their intersections with the picture plane are brought down vertically.

If we now draw through circle points in the plan further horizontal lines parallel to one another in an arbitrary direction up to the picture plane, take their points of intersection on the horizontals through the elevation down into the picture, and then draw lines through the points of intersection in the picture to the vanishing point for the auxiliary lines, then the required images of the circle points will be the points of intersection of these auxiliary vanishing lines with the verticals through the points of intersection of the visual rays and the picture plane. In particular, if we take the parallel auxiliary lines to be perpendicular to the plane intersecting the angle between the picture plane and the circle plane, then the vanishing point of the auxiliary lines will be the measuring point, and the figure obtained from the points of intersection of the auxiliary lines with the picture plane will be a circle.

A High-Pressure Gas-Holder

The sphere, picture plane *PP*, and standpoint *S* are fixed in plan, and the centre of vision *CV* and the diagonal point *D* are determined. The angle of vision for the whole picture is about 30° and the principal visual ray is perpendicular to *PP*.

The points *CV* and *D* are brought down vertically on to the horizon *h* placed parallel to, and below, *PP*; the height of eye, h_e, is marked in, and an elevation—of the sphere and its supporting frame—is drawn in on the same scale as the plan. A depth-line is drawn to *CV* from the sphere centre in the elevation. The nearest and furthest points of the sphere are projected on to *PP* in the plan by lines inclined at 45° and are then brought down vertically on to the horizontal through the sphere centre in the elevation, and from these points lines are drawn to *D*. The points where these lines cut the depth-line through the sphere centre in the elevation are the foci F_1 and F_2 of the image ellipse. The minor axis of the ellipse lies on the perpendicular bisector of the interval F_1F_2. Its length $2b$ is obtained—if the sphere is situated symmetrically relative to *S*, as in our example—as the interval cut off along *PP* by visual rays from *S* tangent to the sphere in the plan. If the sphere is not symmetric relative to *S* in the plan, these tangent rays have to be drawn from a different point *S'*, relative to which the sphere is symmetrically situated; i. e. *S* is shifted to *S'* parallel to the picture plane. The length a of the major semi-axis is equal to the distance of the end of the minor axis from a focus.

The image ellipse can now be drawn as explained on page 18, but drawing it as a compound curve, using the method explained on page 16 (1), saves time and is sufficiently accurate.

The image points for the sloping frame lie on the depth-lines drawn from points in the elevation to *CV* and vertically below the points of intersection of the visual rays from *S* to the corresponding points in the plan with the picture plane *PP*.

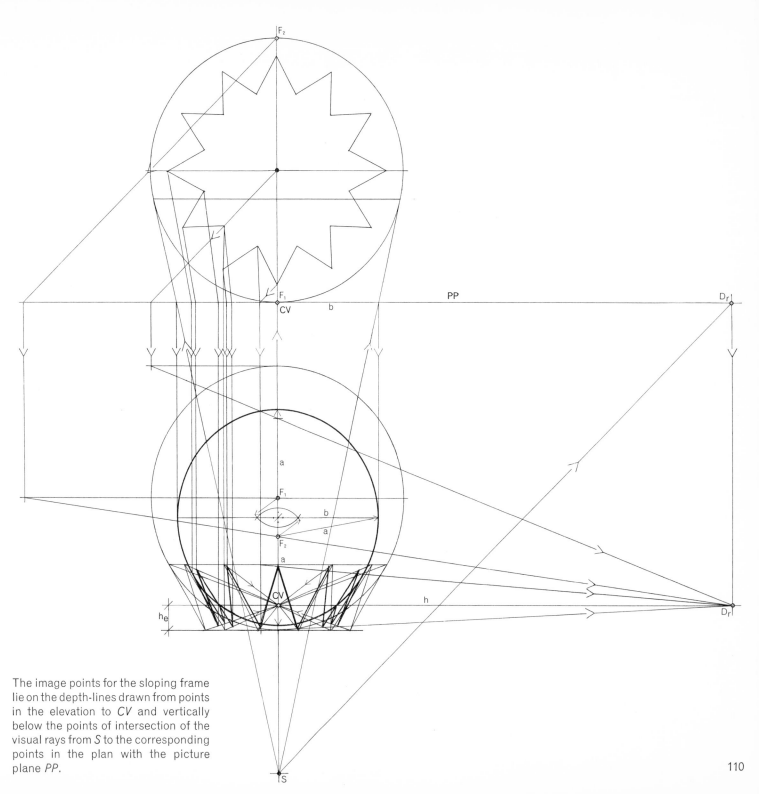

Ball Race

The plan of the object and the positions of the picture plane *PP* and the standpoint (inaccessible in our diagram) are suitably arranged, the auxiliary vanishing point (the half-distance point $\frac{1}{2}D$) is determined, the horizon *h* is taken to be the picture plane trace, and the elevation is set up below it. Depth-lines are drawn to the centre of vision *CV* from the centres of the spheres in the elevation. From the nearest and furthest points of the spheres in the plan, lines are drawn inclined to the depth-lines at a slope of 1:2; these are half-distance lines and their intersections with the picture plane are taken down vertically to the level of the sphere centres in the elevation, and from there the half-distance vanishing lines are drawn to $\frac{1}{2}D$. Their intersections with

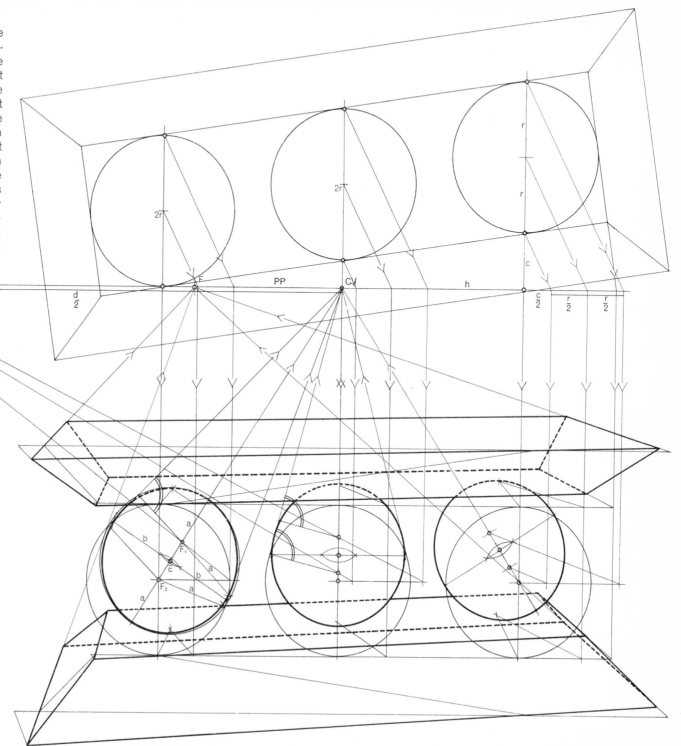

the corresponding depth-lines are the foci of the image ellipses. The construction then proceeds exactly as described on the previous page.

The perspective images of spheres which do not cover the centre of vision *CV* can also be constructed as follows. A pair of tangents is drawn from *CV* to the elevation of the sphere. From one of the foci, say F_1, a perpendicular is dropped on to one of the tangents. Then from the centre of the ellipse, the point *E* midway between F_1 and F_2 (remember that *E* is not the perspective image of the actual centre of the sphere), a circle is drawn through the foot of the perpendicular on the tangent. The radius of this circle is *a*, the major semi-axis of the ellipse; the circle itself is what mathematicians call the auxiliary circle, i.e. it is the circle which just encloses the ellipse. So, on the depth-line through F_1 and F_2, this circle will cut off a length equal to the major axis, 2*a*, of the ellipse. Then circular arcs with radius *a* and centred at F_1 and F_2 will give by their intersections the position and length of the minor axis of the ellipse.

111

Roman Cross-Vaults Viewed Axially

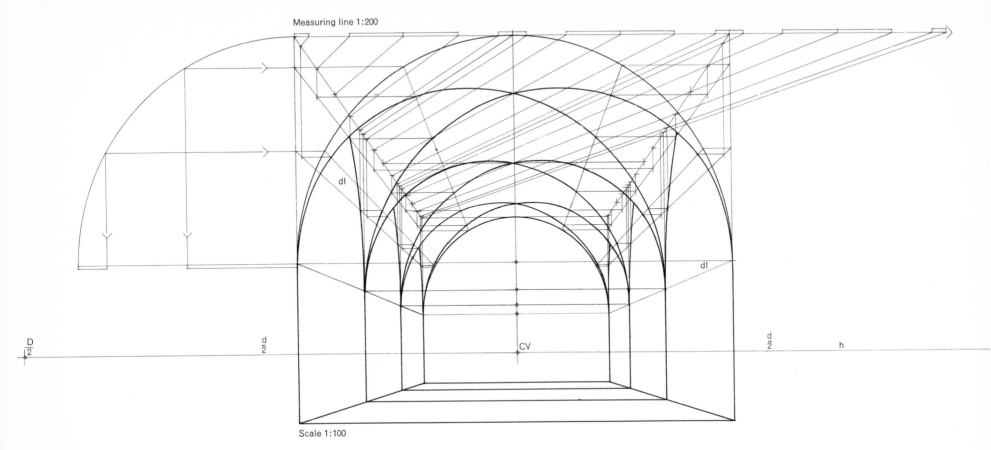

Measuring line 1:200

Scale 1:100

A Roman cross-vault, that is, a half-barrel groined vault formed by the intersection of two perpendicular semi-cylindrical vaults of equal size and height, is drawn here in central perspective by means of measuring lines and half-distance points. We lay down first the intersection of the picture plane with the hemicylinder, the centre of vision, and to left and right of the latter the half-distance points at the distance $d/2$, where d is the chosen distance from the standpoint to the picture plane. Depth-lines and horizontals are drawn through all the important points of the picture plane's intersection with the semi-cylinder. The arc is enclosed in a rectangle whose vertical sides are appropriately subdivided; the semi-cylinder is enclosed in a perspective 'box' formed from this rectangle and depth-lines. Starting from one of the upper corners of the rectangle a measuring line for depths is constructed; the horizontal distances of object points from the picture plane (including any pillars which may exist) are plotted on half the scale used in the plan. Then vanishing lines to the half-distance point cut off the cor-

responding depths along depth-lines. Verticals through these points of subdivision determine on the other depth-lines of the box the various points of the arch on one side; the points of subdivision are transferred horizontally to the other side, and then the points of the arch on this side are determined by means of verticals in the same way. Horizontals drawn from points on the side arches determine on the depth-lines of the hemicylinder itself the positions of points on the diagonal arches. The undistorted circles are drawn first, then the diagonal arches including the side arches, and finally the straight lines are put in.

Diagram on page 113

The $1:\sqrt{2}$ elliptical groins of Roman cross-vaulting are raised to become circular in Romanesque cross-vaulting. The perspective can be constructed in exactly the same way as in the preceding example, using the half-distance points and a measuring line. Since in our diagram the measuring line would not fit into the sheet, the depths

here have been constructed by alternating half-diagonals and horizontals in the abutment plane. The transverse arch, which is parallel to the picture plane and therefore undistorted, has in this case to be drawn in, in contrast to Roman cross-vaulting. The 45° points of the side arches are determined on the left by the intersections of the diagonals in the perspective lateral squares with the depth-lines displaced to that position, and on the right through the intersections of the depth-lines transferred here with the perspective images of the 45°-angled triangles of tangents.

It is generally expedient to carry out the construction for only a few points of the arches but to determine the direction of the curves as well at these points, if possible with the vanishing points, otherwise by representing the pavilion roofs touching the diagonal arches at the constructed points above each of the squares of the vaulting. The vertex of the pavilion roof for the 45° points of the diagonal arcs are obtained by means of 45° lines from the vertices of the side arches.

112

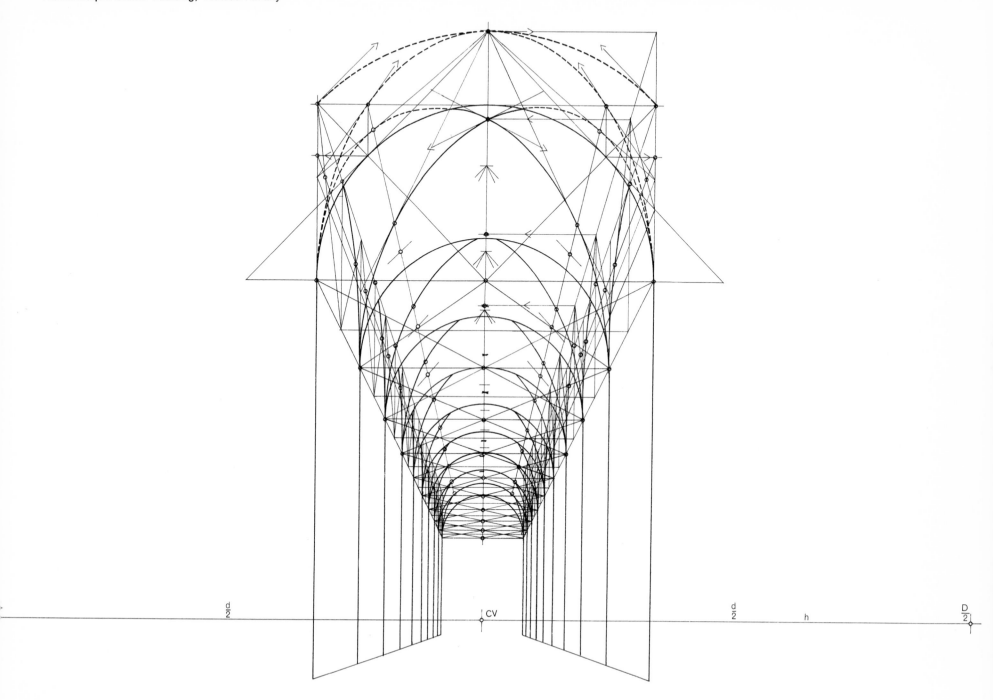

d/2   CV   d/2   h   D/2

Prefabricated Parabolic Arch, Viewed Axially

The drawing is carried out as a central perspective without using a plan but using the half-distance points. The front face of the arch lies in the picture plane and is drawn to the scale 1:400. The span width is 108 m., height of vertex 27 m., and the axial distance between the parabolic members is 12 m. (or in English units, say, $108 \times 27 \times 12$ yards).

The parabola is constructed by the first method described on page 17 by means of an isosceles triangle of double the height, with its equal sides divided into 32 equal parts. The height of eye, h_e, is 2 m. (6 ft.) and the centre of vision is taken to be central. The half-distance points $D/2$ lie to left and right of CV at a distance equal to half the distance from the standpoint to the picture plane. In view of the size and the strongly marked distinctiveness of the elements, an angle of vision of 90° has been adopted; hence the distance d equals half the span width. The rectangle circumscribing the parabola is drawn, and through each point of the parabola horizontals or verticals are drawn to the sides of this rectangle. Depth-lines are drawn through the points of the parabola and through the points of intersection just obtained on the sides of the rectangle. A measuring line for depths, on the scale $\frac{1}{2}:400 = 1:800$, is marked off along the top edge of the rectangle, inwards from each corner. Vanishing lines to

the half-distance points from points on these measuring lines intersect the corresponding depth-lines at the appropriate perspective depths; and the verticals or horizontals through these points give the perspective elevations of the parabolic arches or the perspectively diminishing plans of the areas between parabolic elements respectively. The horizontals drawn in from points of the side elevations or verticals drawn downwards from the perspective plans intersect the depth-lines through points of the parabola in the required points; these must, of course, be joined up to form the remoter parabolas. The drawing is the most accurate if the side elevations are used for constructing points near the vertex of the arches and the perspective plans are used for constructing the points near the bottom of the arches. Notice that, if we think of the parabolas as made up of successive line elements, then all those which in reality are at the same height will be parallel to one another.

Diagram on page 115
For this representation of a similar object to that on page 114 we need the plan, here to scale 1:400, arranged in the desired way relative to the picture plane.

One or two visual rays determine the size of the picture; the standpoint should be centrally in front of the picture. The points of intersection of the object with the picture plane determine the symmetric curve of intersection o of the parabolic object with the picture plane, and a line through the standpoint S parallel to the axis of the object fixes the vanishing point V.

The points thus determined are brought down vertically on to the horizon h or on to lines parallel to h plotted, on the scale 1:400, at the relevant heights above or below h. The parabola is drawn by the method explained on page 19, using a triangle with two of its sides divided into 32 equal parts. The measuring points M_1 and M_2 are fixed to left and right of the vanishing point at the distance equal to one half the distance from the standpoint S to the vanishing point V. The parabola is enclosed in a rectangle and depth-lines are drawn through the various points of the rectangle and the parabola. On the upper side of the rectangle measuring lines are plotted on the scale 1:800 for the depths of object points; these scales start from the corners of the rectangle, and depths into the picture increase inwards while depths of points in front of the picture plane are measured outwards from the corner of the rectangle. Straight lines from the measuring points M_1 and M_2 to these scales cut the depth-

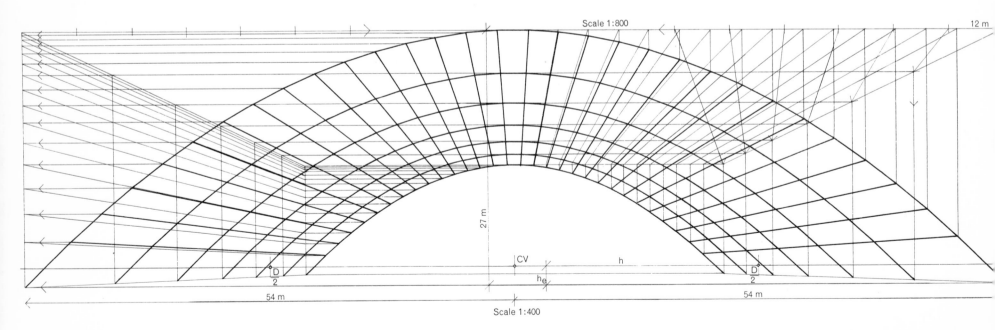

Scale 1:800 ... 12 m ... 27 m ... CV ... h ... h_e ... $\frac{D}{2}$ ... 54 m ... 54 m ... Scale 1:400

Parabolic Arch Viewed Slightly Diagonally

lines in the corresponding perspective depths. Joined together, these points of intersection give the divisions for depth along the vertices of the arches, and brought down vertically they give the divisions for depth along the bottom edges of the archway. By drawing verticals through the depth divisions along the vertices of the arches we obtain the depth divisions along the ridge of the auxiliary figure. The straight lines joining ridge points to the corresponding base points yield triangles, whose sides can be divided into 32 equal parts by lines from *V* to the points of subdivision on the triangle round *o*. Then, using method (2) of page 19, the elements of the parabolic arches can be drawn in between the vanishing lines of the arch.

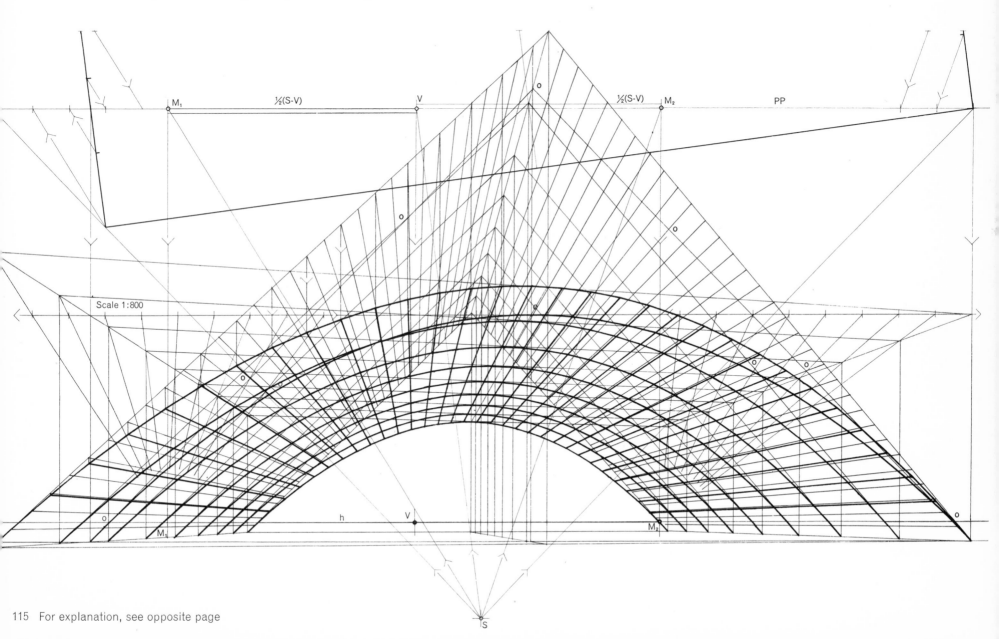

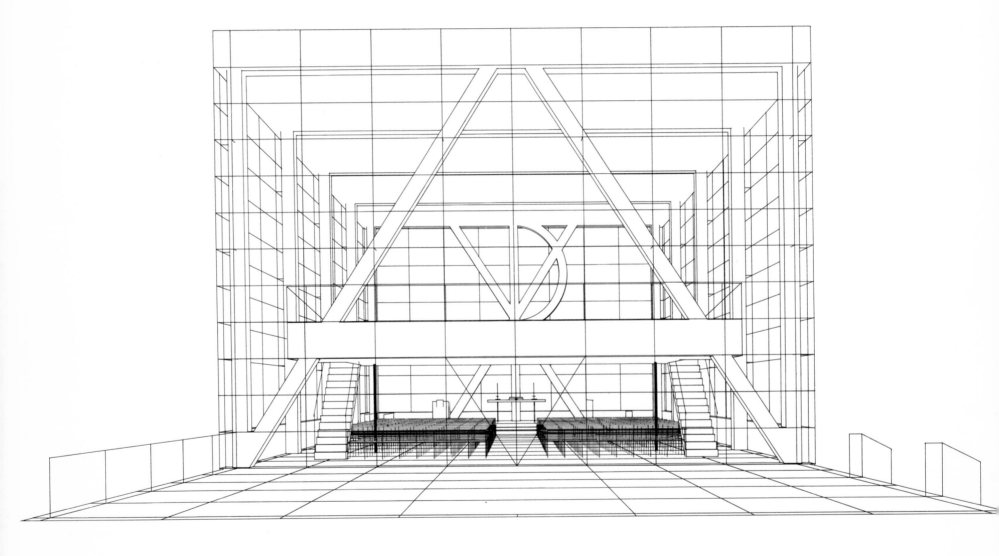

Central perspective

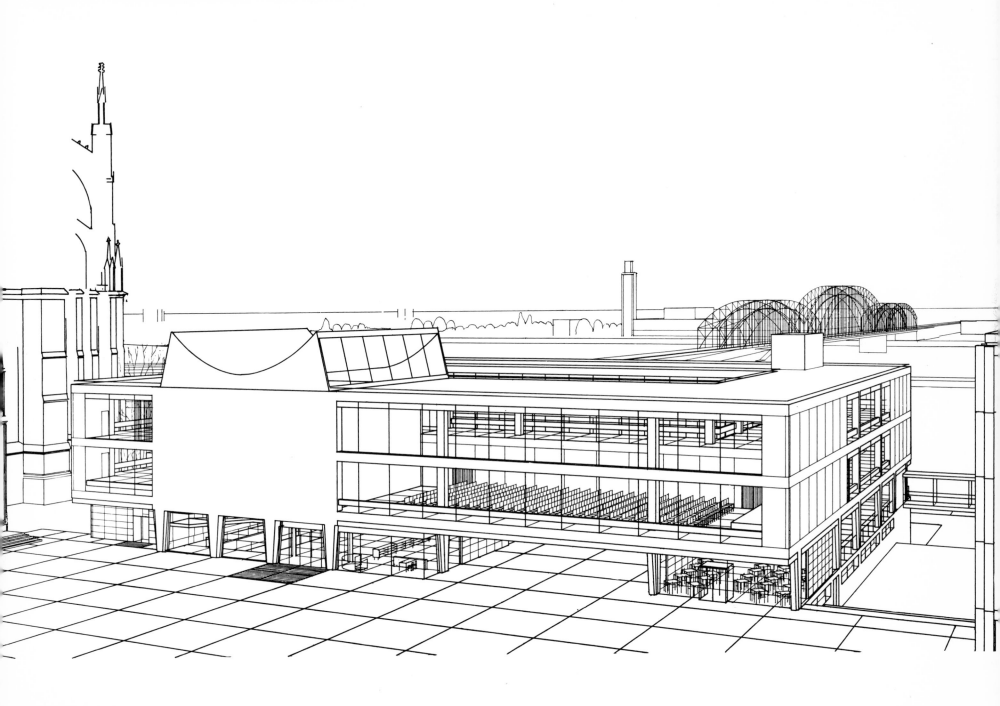

Perspective drawn using radial arms; reproduced on a
reduced scale.

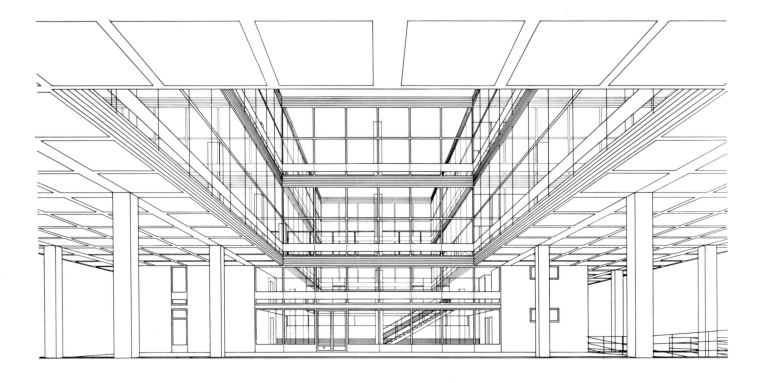

Central perspective drawn without using the plan; reproduced on a reduced scale. In this perspective drawing the angle of vision has been taken larger than has
been recommended elsewhere in this book, in order to
show the whole of the opposite façade of the inner court.

Design for an art gallery in Düsseldorf; exterior view

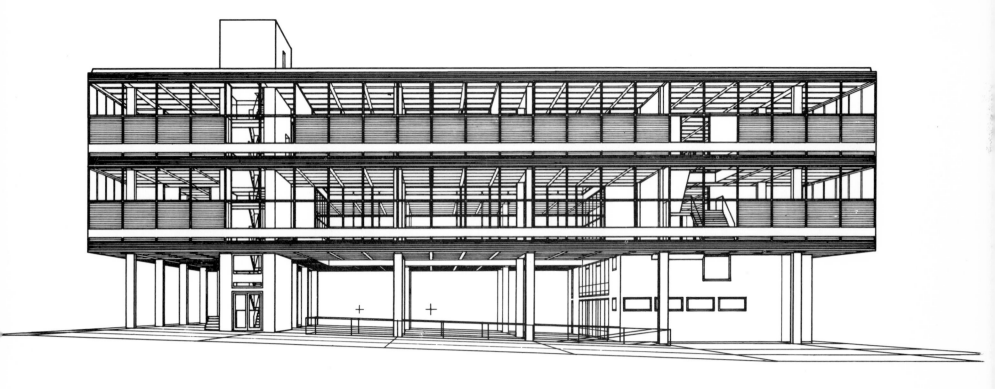

Central perspective drawn without using the plan; reproduced on a reduced scale.